STOCK MARKET 2021

DAY TRADING

STRATEGIES FOR NEW DAY TRADERS, TO BUY AND GAIN THE BEST PASSIVE INCOME AND FINANCIAL FREEDOM

Robert Taegan

© Copyright 2020 by Robert Taegan All rights reserved.

This content is provided with the sole purpose of providing relevant information on a specific topic, for which every reasonable effort has been made to ensure that it is both accurate and reasonable. Nevertheless, by purchasing this content, you consent to the fact that the author, as well as the publisher, are in no way experts on the topics contained herein, regardless of any claims as such that may be made within. As such, any suggestions or recommendations that are made within are done so purely for entertainment value. It is recommended that you always consult a professional prior to undertaking any advice or techniques discussed within this book. This is a legally binding declaration that is considered both valid and fair by the Committee of Publishers Association and the American Bar Association, and should be considered as legally binding within the United States. The reproduction, transmission, and duplication of any of the content found herein, including any specific or extended information will be considered an illegal act regardless of the end form the information ultimately takes. This includes copied versions of the work—physical, digital, and audio—unless express consent of the Publisher is sought beforehand. Any additional rights reserved. Furthermore, the information that can be found within the pages described forthwith shall be considered both accurate and truthful when it comes to the recounting of facts. As such, any use, correct or incorrect, of the provided information will render the Publisher free of responsibility as to the actions taken outside of their direct purview. Regardless, there are zero scenarios where the original author or the Publisher can be deemed liable in any fashion for any damages or hardships that may result from any of the information discussed herein. Additionally, the information in the following pages is intended only for informational purposes, and should thus be thought of as universal. As befitting its nature, it is presented without assurance regarding its prolonged validity or interim quality. Trademarks, that are mentioned, are done without written consent and can in no way be considered an endorsement from the trademark holder.

TABLE OF CONTENTS

Introduction 1

Chapter 1: What is Stock Market Trading: Benefits and Disadvantages 4

    What are Stocks? 4
    What Are the Benefits of Trading on The Stock Market? 6
        Investment Gains 6
        Gaining Dividends 6
        Passive Income 6
        Savings 7
        Return on Investment 7
        Retirement 8
        Dividends and Capital Gains 9
        Power to Cast A Ballot 9
        Expansion 10
    How the Stock Market Works 10

Chapter 2: Stock, Bonds and Companies (Corporations and Taxes) 12

    Bonds 12
        Bond Issuers 14
        Comparison with Stocks 14
        Primary Bond Categories 17
            Government bonds 17
            Corporate bonds 17
            Municipal bonds 17
            Agency bonds 17
    Stocks 18
        Most Typical Forms of Stocks 19
            Common Stock 19
            Preferred Stock 19
        Be Aware of the Costs of Investing in Stocks 20

  Tax Implications 20
  Tax on Dividends 20
  Tax on Capital Gains 21
 Taxation and Bonds 21
  Wash Sales and Tax Losses 22
  Opportunity Cost 22

Chapter 3: How to Start Trading and What Do You Need Before You Start 24

 Things to Consider Before Investing in A Stock 24
  Plan the Investment 24
  Plan Your Investment Strategies 24
  Draw the Investment Plan You Just Made 25
  Learn the Difference Between Investing and Speculating .. 25
  Understand the Importance of Timing (And the Impossibility of Getting It Right) 25
 How to Invest in the Stock Market? 26
  Determine Your Financial Goals 26
  Open a Retirement Account 26
  Choose a Stockbroker 27
  Begin with Mutual Funds 27
  Invest in Index Funds 27
  Use Dollar-Cost Averaging Method 28
  Educate Yourself About Investments 28
  Go into Direct Stock Investments Gradually 29
  Monitor Your Portfolio 29
  Always Diversify! 30

Chapter 4: Techniques and Strategies That Will Help You 31

 Value Investing 31
 Growth Investing 31
 Day trading 32
 Position Trading 32

Swing Trading 32
Scalping 33
Index fund investing 33
Dollar-cost Averaging 34
Averaging down 34

Chapter 5: How Does Dividend Investing Works and How to Start with Profits and Risks 35

What Are Dividends? 35
When to Reinvest or Not to Reinvest 36
How to Start Chasing Dividend Income 37
  Pick a Type of Account 37
  Choose a Stockbroker 38
  Decide between ETFs and Stocks 38
  Keep on Contributing and Investing 38
Creating Passive Income with Dividend Stocks 39
How to Generate a Passive Income Annually from Dividend Stocks 40
  Track Record 40
  Management Focus 40
  Company Type 41
  Diversification 41
  High Yields 42
  Long-Term Hold 42

Chapter 6: How to Set Your Portfolio 43

The Most Effective Method to Fabricate A Wise Investment Portfolio 43
  Have A Ton of Fun with Your Portfolio 44
  Building an Investment Portfolio 45
Principles of Building A Portfolio 45
How to Build a Portfolio of Stocks to Invest in 46

    Determine the Asset Allocation That You Think Is Suitable for You 47
    Create Your Portfolio According to Your Design 47
    Rebalance Your Portfolio 47

Chapter 7: How to Evaluate and Compare Stocks 49

    Various Types of Stocks 49
        Common Stock Shares 49
        Preferred Stocks 49
        Custom Stock Classes 50
        Warrant Stocks 50
    What Determines Stock Price? 50

Chapter 8: Beginners' Mistakes That Should Be Avoided 52

    Poor Preparation: "If you fail to plan, then you are planning to fail" cit 52
    Being Emotional 53
    Anticipating Returns and scaling up your shares size to quick 53
    Dependence on Tools 54

Chapter 9: What Is Meant By Day trading And How It Operates 55

    What Is Day trading? 55
    How Day trading Works 56

Chapter 10: The Meaning And Importance of Volume, Price, And Technical Indicators 60

    How Is Stock Price Determined? 60
    Technical Indicators 61

Chapter 11: Risk and Account Management in Day Trading 63

    Risk Management 63
        Assessing Your Risk Tolerance 64
        The Dangers of Ignoring Risk Tolerance 65

 Volatility Risks 65

 Geopolitical Events 66

 Economic Events 66

 Inflation 66

Strategies for Managing Volatility 67

 Always invest in stocks whose dividends rise Consistently 67

 Timing Risks 67

 Dollar-Cost Averaging 67

Chapter 12: Examples of Day Trades, Advice and Methods That Beginners Should Know 69

Profitable Stocks for the Best Investor 69

Dividend Growth Investing: Case Study 71

Investment Criteria for Top Stocks 71

How to Succeed in the Stock Market? 73

Chapter 13: How to Buy Your First Stock 74

Picking Out Stocks to Invest In 74

 Pick A Sector That Is Doing Well 74

 Growing Profits 74

 The Size of Your Company 75

 Look at The Dividend Payments 75

 Manageable Debt 75

 Go with Liquid Stocks 76

Buying Your First Stock 76

 Finding A Brokerage 76

 Research Stocks 77

Buying Your First Stock 77

 Market Order 78

 Limit Order 78

 Stop Order 78

 Stop Limit Order 79

 Trailing Stop Order 79

Chapter 14: How to Generate Passive Income in The Stock Market 80

How to Make Money in the Stock Market 80
Determine Why You Want to Sell 81
Take Full Advantage of Time 81
Practice Investing Regularly 81
Maintain a Portfolio That Is Diverse 82
Get Help From A Professional 82

Chapter 15: How to Spot A Stock That Is About to Explode Higher 83

Price/Earnings (P/E) Ratio 84
Earnings Yield 84
The Essence of Value Investing 85

Chapter 16: How to trade momentum stocks 87

What are momentum stocks? 87
Why People Choose Momentum Investing 87
The Advantages of Trading Momentum Stocks 87
The Downsides of Trading Momentum Stocks 88
Momentum Stock Trading - Entry Points Are Tips to Earn from Momentum Trading 90
How to Spot the Best Momentum Stocks 90
How to Sight Momentum Stocks 91
Exit Strategies for Momentum Stocks 92
Momentum Stock Trading - Stop-losses Are Essential to Capital Preservation 93
How to Set an Effective Stop-loss 94

Chapter 17: Insider Tricks Used by Professional Traders 95

Maximizing Your Investments 95
Retirement Plans 95

Do Not Follow the Crowd 96
Pick Out A Strategy and Always Stick with It 96
Forget About the Timing 96
Only Invest What You Can Afford 97
Keep Your Expectations Realistic 97
Keep the Emotions Out of The Game 97
Set Your Stop Points 98
Focus on Price 98
Practice Before You Jump In 98
Always Have A Plan and Stick to It 99
Do Your Research 99
Treat It as A Business 99
Be A Continuous Learner 99
Do Not Risk What You Cannot Afford to Lose 100
Always Use A Stop-loss 100
Know When to Stop 100
Avoid the Herd Mentality 100
Have a Financial Plan 101
Be Clear on What to Buy and What to Sell 101
Stay Focused 101
Develop in You the Intelligent State of Mind 102
Have a Trading Plan 102
Make the Best Use of Technology 102
Keep a Check on Economic Calendars 103
Always Practice 103
Observe the Habits of Successful Trades 103
Give Considerable Thought Before Choosing Your
Trading Style 104
Choose the Right Broker 104
Do not Try to Outsmart the Markets 104

Chapter 18: Analysis of the stocks 106

Bull and Bear Markets 106
Fundamental Analysis 107
   Steps to Fundamental Evaluation *110*
      Determine the Stock or Security 110
      Economic Forecast 110
      Company Analysis 111
      Business Model 112
      Competitive Advantage 112
      Management 113
      Industry factors 114
      Government policy 115
      Market share 115
      Industry growth 115
   Fundamental Analysis Example 2020 .... *116*
Technical Analysis 116
   Factors Affecting Technical Analysis *117*
   Examine the Charts *118*
   Cup-with-Handle Pattern *119*
   Charting Varying Time Frames *120*
   How to Read Charts *121*
   Why are Stock Charts Valuable? *121*
   Stock Chart Interpretation *122*
      Price 122
      Volumes 122
   Moving Averages *122*
   Comparing Stock Market Indices *123*
   Two Popular Stock Market Indices *124*
   How to Conduct the Indexes Comparison *124*

Chapter 19: Possible Suggestion on How to Find A Profitable Stock Investment After the Pandemic 127

Analyze Your Stock Before You Buy It 127
   Study the Company's Revenues *128*

Check the Company's Gross Profit Margin Or GPM 128
Analyze the Company Debt 129
Evaluate Return on Equity (ROE) 130
Study the Company's Earnings Growth 130
Find Out the Company's Price-To-Earnings (P/E) Ratio 131
Make A Comparison Table 131
Great Stocks to Buy and Hold in 2020 132

Chapter 20: How the Market Will Suffer After Coronavirus and How They Can Get Back on Track 133

The Fluctuating Stock Prices 134
Why is it Difficult to Predict? 134
Stock Valuation 135
Triggering Event 136
The Human Decision Process 136
Important Reminders 137

Conclusion 139

Note of the Author 142

INTRODUCTION

The stock market has a certain appeal that never fails to entice a person. However, not everyone would dare try their luck in investing, due to its equally intimidating aura. The truth is, it is not that difficult to understand the ins and outs of stock market, although the actual engagement may be a bit tricky.

This book contains what you need to know to get started as it will answer almost every question that people ask about the stock market without any hype or promises. It provides practical steps on how you can get started and how you can make good decisions.

The following chapters will discuss stock marketing in detail, with beginners' perspective in mind. We will also discuss different technical analysis methods that will help us understand how stock markets really work, and principles we need to adapt to succeed. It is a known fact that markets are random and predicting it just a mere myth. Even so, understand the fact that randomness can be analyzed if we have a lot of known parameters. If you have a lot of real-time knowledge about factors affecting stock you bought, you will easily know whether to hold it or not.

For the investors who are preparing to invest in stocks, the basic methods of learning how to open an account, watching the market, and mastering computer and mobile phone stock apps is an extremely important compulsory course. The correct stock trading skills can improve the accuracy of the forecast of stock price trend, thus directly affecting the success or failure of an investor's investment.

To this end, through continuous summarization and practice, we have compiled this book. From the practical point of view, this book will have the necessary knowledge of how to watch the market. The actual application of investing skills of stocks that need to be mastered enables the investors to apply them to the actual stock market investment, and gain income after learning the relevant methods.

This book carefully selects the most practical methods and techniques of stock investment to focus on. First, there is entry knowledge; then, the four actual combats; then the six major analyses; and finally, the description of a process that is an easy comprehensible way to describe and explain the entire knowledge structure.

There are countless techniques and methods for stock investment. The ones listed in this book are comprehensive. Although this book only touches upon the basics, it serves as a great introductory source creating a good foundation and provides the best practices that traders and investors follow to be successful. It even gives the different ways you can approach the stock market that would suit your goals and risk tolerance.

After reading this book, you will be equipped with the required knowledge to start your journey towards a better financial future. You will know what you need to avoid, so you do not make stupid and costly mistakes. Lastly, you will increase your chances of achieving the financial goals that would greatly benefit yourself, your family, and your loved ones.

CHAPTER 1

What Is Stock Market Trading: Benefits And Disadvantages

What are Stocks?

To understand what stocks are, we need to define shares. A **share** is a unit of ownership in a company. A company's capital is often divided into equal portions of shares. Anyone who owns company shares is known as a shareholder. A shareholder gets to share in decision-making and the profits generated by the company.

Stock refers to 100 units of shares. Therefore, shareholders are also referred to as stock-owners. A company's shares are sold and bought in the form of stock. Stock simply means units of ownership bundled into units of 100.

Stocks allow investors and generally members of the public to claim part ownership of a company, however small this ownership may be. Companies often sell stocks to the public to raise funds for their operations. In return, buyers get to own a small part of the company depending on the number of shares held.

Stocks carry a price because they can be sold or bought at the secondary markets. This price is based on a number of factors include the company's earnings. Positive news regarding a good financial performance, expansion, a renowned CEO, etc. often has a positive effect on the price. When the company performs poorly, the stock price is likely to fall. Therefore, the price of stocks depends on factors such as a company's profits, the general performance of the economy and positive news regarding the company. Negative news affects the company's stock negatively.

Does it also mean that you have the right to explore or access the areas within the company that are supposed to be off-limits to unauthorized persons? Can you just grab anything that the company owns, like a table or printer, just because you also own a part of it? Do you have the right to hire or fire workers?

Many investment experts claimed that a stock embodies a shareholder's claim on the company's earnings and assets. They further added that when you buy more stocks of that company, the percentage of your ownership also increases. Regrettably, the definition of stock that many investment experts believe to be accurate has some flaws, and therefore is not entirely correct.

Just remember that you only own a small portion of the company, and such ownership does not give you any authority to do things as you please with the company. Even if you own a significant number of shares, you only have the right to vote when there is a major decision that concerns all shareholders of that company.

What Are the Benefits of Trading on The Stock Market?

Investment Gains

The clearest advantage of buying or selling stocks is investment gains. It is the possibility of developing wealth through valuation of resources (stocks) that first attracts most people to invest in the stock market, with an end goal to make sure about their monetary future.

Gaining Dividends

A few stocks additionally offer the chance to procure dividends. Dividends can be an extraordinary method to acquire transient investment income. Frankly, who does not need another income stream?

Passive Income

In a nutshell, passive income is something that generates money on a regular basis without the need to oversee it regularly. You do not even need to exert too much effort to create and maintain it. However, it is still advisable to conduct minimum monitoring to make sure that nothing is amiss.

You can make an upfront investment in terms of time and/or money, just to start things up. Once the ball starts rolling, you just practically need to wait and then collect your earnings later.

Stocks are great for passive income. However, you need to choose wisely when buying stocks. Do not buy on impulse following a friend's suggestion (without any knowledge about stocks), or let your loyalty to a certain product or company cloud your judgment. You are looking for something that can bring you a lot of advantages, not for a way to display your devotion to a certain product. If the company that manufactures your favorite product has a good stock market standing, then buy some stocks if they offer them.

Savings

Saving money means setting aside a fixed or variable amount of money on a regular basis (every pay day), or whenever you have excess cash on hand. You may keep it in a bank, your home vault, piggy bank, or other safe places. You can also use your money to buy stocks and turn it into savings.

When you invest, you use the money to buy an asset that you think is safe to acquire and can bring you acceptable rate of return. Some of the most productive investments are real estate, bonds, and stocks. The good thing about buying stock is that you do not need a large sum of money to buy it. There are good stocks that you can buy without the need to spend so much.

Return on Investment

ROI or return on investment measures the amount of return on your chosen investment against the cost of investment. It can help the investor evaluate the investment's efficiency. The investor can also draft a chart to see the efficiency of his/her investments, and compare them with one another. You can use this formula to get the ROI:

$$ROI = \frac{\text{Earnings from Investment} - \text{Investment Cost}}{\text{Investment Cost}}$$

The **earnings from investment** in the above formula pertains to the acquired proceeds from the sale of investment. The **investment cost** is the total price that the investor paid for a particular investment, such as stocks. The difference that you will get from the two is the benefit or return. When you divide that by **investment cost**, you will get the ROI that is expressed in percentage form.

Retirement

When you are in your twenties, retirement is probably the last thing you can think of. However, it is undeniable that making early preparations for your retirement is an excellent financial move.

You need to properly balance everything. If you spend all your time focusing on finding ways to save more money and providing value, you will not have a chance to enjoy the fruits of your labor to the fullest. On the other hand, if you do not save enough money or failed to provide value, you will not get to do much with your time.

Dividends and Capital Gains

A stockholder may get earnings, which are delivered as dividends. The organization can choose the frequency of dividend payments; it can be either be in regular periods (for example, one quarter or one year), or the company can choose to hold the entirety of the earnings to grow the business further. Besides dividends, the stockholder can appreciate capital increases from stock price appreciation.

Power to Cast A Ballot

Another incredible element of stock possession is that investors are qualified to vote in favor of an executive's changes if the organization is underperforming. The official leading body of an organization will hold yearly gatherings to report general organization execution. They unveil plans for future tasks and the nominations of executives. Should investors and stockholders contradict the organization's current activity or tentative arrangements, they can arrange changes to be made in the board or business procedure.

Limited Liability

Finally, when an individual claims shares of an organization, the nature of possession is constrained. Should the organization fail, investors are not at risk of any misfortune.

Expansion

We should not disregard expansion, which is another significant advantage of investing in the stock market that is ignored by many. An appropriately differentiated investment portfolio permits losses in a single division of the market to be balanced by gains in another, which means the portfolio can be profitable overall.

How the Stock Market Works

Most stocks are traded in the various stock exchanges in the world. These exchanges are regulated by the government agencies responsible for securities and exchanges in the host countries. The government agencies protect those investing in the publicly listed companies from financial fraud, and help maintain the operation of the stock exchanges.

There are three major players in the stock market : the investment banks, stockbrokers, and investors. The investment banks are responsible for handling the **initial public offering (IPO)** of companies when they decide to offer their shares for public investment. These banks are approached by companies and become their underwriters. As an **underwriter,** the investment bank will use its research on the company to determine the guaranteed minimum price per share, and how much of the ownership the company can relinquish to the public as shares. In return, the investment bank handles the initial issue of shares to the public for a fee. Usually, large institutional investors, like mutual fund companies, purchase shares sold during an IPO. After that, all trading of the shares occurs in the stock exchange – the secondary market.

In the exchange, stockbrokers buy and sell the stocks according to the order of their clients – the investors. Stockbrokers might also act as financial advisors, so that their clients make the best decisions according to their goals. They often offer research on publicly traded companies and provide a forecast on overall market index or stock price performance. This service is offered since stockbrokers want their clients to succeed in their investments and trades. If they experience success in their stock trades, they will more likely transact more trades and remain as their costumer.

CHAPTER 2

Stock, Bonds and Companies
(Corporations and Taxes)

Bonds

Bonds have been in existence since time immemorial. They were used by ancient governments to raise money for various capital-intensive causes, as done even today. So, what exactly are bonds? In the stock trading sense of the word, a **bond** is like a unit of a bigger loan that a company or government takes from a large pool of investors for a specific purpose. The whole loan, thus taken, also falls under the definition of a bond. What individual investors hold in their hands as the bond, is usually the certificate given to signify the borrowing relationship they enter into with the borrower. According to the bond certificate, the terms of payment and details of the loan are indicated, including the interest rate and maturity date. Trading in bonds can either be over the counter in the bourse, or directly between lender and borrower.

The system of bond borrowing can be traced way back to the ancient Mesopotamian financial systems, where corporations borrowed grain with the promise to pay back the principal plus interest at a certain date. Instead of placing the company assets as surety, a bond was used instead, symbolizing the borrower's deepest commitment to repay the loan. As financial systems evolved, this obligation to repay the debt came to represent the bond the current world knows. Bonds are necessitated by a number of realities that only the insider might know about the capital markets.

The capital requirements of large corporations are quite extensive. To start a new project, to finance ongoing operations (especially in research and development), and to repay old debts that have not been repaid yet, companies need to raise massive amounts of money. From large infrastructural projects to militaristic efforts, governments have an appetite for capital that is tax remissions from citizens and businesses do not meet.

In some cases, the banks cannot meet the demand simply because the amount of money these entities require is huge. The risk of a bank going under, in the event of these massive borrowers defaulting is too great. This means that corporations and governments have to be creative about how they raise the money for their critical requirements.

Bonds are considered to be quite conservative as investment options, mostly because the possibility of losing one's money is low. Short of going out of business, bond issuers repay their debt obligations in full; and even in the event of going bankrupt, bondholders are treated as creditors, and are paid first from the liquefied assets of a company. Governments absolutely pay their bonds, sometimes issuing a new bond just to repay the old.

Bond Issuers

The three main entities that issue bonds are corporations, municipals, and governments. The government is the major bond issuer, responsible for more than 50% of all bonds floating around in the stock market. The treasury issues bonds on behalf of the government, with the word assigned to them, varying by their maturity rate.

Bonds that are expected to mature within the year are defined as **bills**. Instruments that mature within ten years of being issued are known as **notes**. Instruments that are expected to mature ten to twenty years after their issue are known simply as **bonds**. The more conventional name for all three categories of government-issued bonds is **treasuries**.

It is not uncommon to hear them all being referred to as treasury bills, treasury notes, and treasury bonds, respectively. Local governments issue bonds to raise money for certain development projects. Because these bonds are unfamiliar and investors are often unsure whether the issuer can actually pay up, the coupon income is often specified as being tax-free, in a bid to attract more investors.

Comparison with Stocks

The main difference between bonds and stocks is that stocks represent a stake in the business, while a bond is essentially a credit service an investor extends to the company or the government. The only reason corporate entities and governments issue bonds is to raise money, while stocks may also be issued to comply with government regulations.

While the money raised during an IPO goes a long way to boost the company's operations, it is often held as liquid assets, because an IPO is simply a matter of a business going public to increase its legitimacy and boost public confidence in its products. An initial public offering is a statement that a company is past the startup stage. A bond issue means nothing more than the fact that a company needs money for operations and wishes to borrow it.

Another area where stocks and bonds differ is in maturity. While bonds come with a pre-arranged maturity date, stocks are perpetual securities. One can hold on to a stock for as long as they wish, collecting dividends on their investment for as long as a whole century. The longest maturity time for a bond is about 30–50 years.

The way that investors make money from either a stock or a bond also differs. With a stock, the price appreciates over time, raising the purported value of an investment (the money a person would make if they sold their shares at this exact moment). This rise in price is determined by **the laws of demand and supply,** such that when the market perceives the company as being healthy financially, the price rises because there is greater demand. The opposite is true when the company is struggling financially and enjoys little confidence in the stock market.

From an investment perspective, stocks and bonds differ in one key area: the perception of security. A stock is viewed as a volatile investment because its price is likely to drop at any time. Even though the overall interest rate of publicly traded companies remains in the low double digits, some perform very badly, and often go into the negative for protracted periods of time. This volatility makes it extremely hard to predict the return that an investment will bring.

For a bond, the interest rate is predetermined and mostly fixed, save for slight deviations, depending on the state of the economy and interest rates. A bond is considered to be safe and conservative, bringing a stabilizing effect to an investment portfolio. Stocks, on the other hand, come with high risk and high reward, and tend to make a portfolio substantially more unpredictable.

Companies that need to raise money can borrow from banks or issue bonds. You should now know that bonds are different from stocks. Shareholders are part-owners (through stocks) of the company, while bondholders are the creditors (not banks) to the company. The bondholders are entitled to charge interest and to receive repayment of principal, a benefit shareholders do not enjoy.

In the event of company bankruptcy, the creditors (banks and/or bondholders) must be paid first before anyone else, as stated under the law. The company is compelled to sell its assets in order to compensate the creditors. The shareholders have the least priority, and often get nothing.

Primary Bond Categories

Government bonds

These are issued by the government, and they are backed by the treasury. Government bonds with less than a year to maturity are called bills, those with a maturity of one to ten years are called notes, and those with more than 10 years maturity are called bonds. These are also known as **sovereign debt**.

Corporate bonds

These are issued by companies. Corporate bonds offer more favorable terms and interest rates than bank loans.

Municipal bonds

These are bonds issued by cities, states, counties, and municipalities. Municipal bonds are used to pay for general obligation and developments projects sponsored by the local government. In some cases, the bond is issued as debt on behalf of non-profit hospitals or colleges.

Agency bonds

These bonds are issued by government-affiliated organizations. Agency bonds come in two types: federal government agency bonds and government-sponsored enterprise bonds.

Federal agency government bonds include those issued by the Government National Mortgage Association, Small Business Administration, and the Federal Housing Administration. These bonds are backed by the government's treasury, but are less liquid compared to government bonds.

Stocks

Stocks are a type of investment instrument that represents a portion of a corporation's ownership and the rights that come along with it. A company initiates the sale of stock to raise capital for business growth or expansion. Those purchasing a company's stock are given a portion of the ownership, depending on how many units they bought, and how this number relates to the number of shares issued by the company.

Ownership of the company's stock gives an investor the right to receive a portion of the business' profits. They also have voting rights, in proportion to the percentage of the company's shares they own, when it comes to board membership and other business decisions requiring input from stockholders.

Holders of a company's stock have limited liability on the company's obligations. This prevents debtors and regulators from chasing after the assets of a company's investors when the business becomes bankrupt and still has outstanding debt. The worst that can happen to investors owning this financial instrument is the complete loss of their investment due to shares losing value.

The terms 'shares' and 'stocks' are often used interchangeably when referring to this financial instrument. 'Stock' is used when referring to shares of a certain company or to the financial instrument. On the other hand, 'shares' is also used as a unit of measurement when referring to a particular amount of the instrument.

Most Typical Forms of Stocks

Common Stock

When you hear people discuss stocks, they are usually discussing common stock. Most companies issue common stocks. In fact, a great majority of stocks are issued in this form.

When you buy a common stock, you can claim profits in form of dividends (a quarterly or a monthly payment to the shareholder of the stock), and you also have the right to vote. You are entitled to one vote per share, to elect the board members.

Over time, common stock may yield higher returns compared to corporate bonds. However, it is riskier to invest in common stock because the shareholder may lose a large portion of the investment when the company happens to go out of business. The common stockholders get the least priority when the company goes bankrupt, and that means they need to wait until the creditors and preferred stockholders get paid. Usually, there are little funds (or none at all) left to be shared among common stockholders.

Preferred Stock

Preferred stocks are similar to bonds. Preferred stockholders have no voting rights, although there are companies that may offer the same privileges that common stockholders enjoy.

Preferred stock investors usually get a fixed dividend. Common stock investors get variable dividends (sometimes high, low, or nothing at all), as declared by the board of directors. The company may also choose to re-purchase the preferred stock shares from the stockholders at any time. Preferred stock shareholders are usually offered a premium price.

In the event of liquidation, preferred stock shareholders are next in line, after the creditors have been paid off. You can think of preferred stocks as a mix of common shares and bonds.

Common stocks and preferred shares are the typical forms of stocks issued by most companies. It is also possible for companies to create a different form or type of stock to meet the requirements of their investors.

The most typical reason of most companies in creating share classes is to congregate the voting power within a particular group. Different classes of shares have different voting privileges.

Be Aware of the Costs of Investing in Stocks

Tax Implications

Aside from investment income, the federal government also taxes dividends, capital gains, real estate, and more. If you earn from a transaction, it is best to expect that you need to pay a certain tax.

Tax on Dividends

The dividend that you receive may be taxed at the rates that apply to either long-term capital gain income or ordinary rates for income. If you are a shareholder of a qualified foreign corporation or a domestic corporation, your dividends will be taxed according to the rates that long-term capital gains need to pay. The dividends that most companies pay are after-tax profits, and it means that the taxman has taken a cut already. The shareholders need not to worry about the 15% preferential tax rate on qualified dividends, if the company is headquartered in the USA. The same goes for companies outside of the country, except for companies that have a double-taxation agreement with the USA.

Non-qualified dividends, which are paid by foreign entities or companies, are income tax-deductible. The tax percentage is usually higher for them.

Tax on Capital Gains

Tax on capital gains depends on the length of time that the investor has the security in his possession. If it is a long-term investment (one year and above), the tax rate is 15%. However, taxpayers with a higher income must pay 20%. Taxpayers who fall in the high-tax bracket should also pay the healthcare surtax. All in all, they need to pay 23.8%.

Short-term investment (less than one year) must pay according to regular income tax rates.

Taxation and Bonds

An investor does not need to pay capital gain tax, if he or she buys a bond at par value and holds it until it matures. However, the investor must pay the tax rate of either long-term or short-term capital gain when he sells the bond and he obtains profit from the sale before it matures–the same with stock.

Corporate bond interest payments are subject to state and federal taxes. Federal bond interest payments are subject to federal taxes, but free from state tax.

Wash Sales and Tax Losses

As an investor, you may offset capital gains against capital losses acquired in the same taxable year or from the previous years. Each year, an individual may deduct net capital losses of $3,000 maximum against other taxable income.

When you harvest tax losses, you can reduce your capital gains tax liability. If your portfolio has one or more stocks that drop below your cost basis, you can sell and achieve a capital loss for tax purposes.

However, there is a catch. The IRS regards the sale and repurchase of a largely similar security within a month as a **wash sale**, which disallows entry of capital loss in the present tax year.

Opportunity Cost

Opportunity cost is a benefit that an individual could have obtained, but let it slip through his fingers in favor of another course of action. It represents a renounced alternative when a certain decision is made. In investing, it is the return difference between the investment that you decided to pass up, and the one that you have chosen.

The different measures that can help you determine the profitability of certain investments were already discussed. When you are already in stock market investing for quite some time, there may be some investments that you thought to be profitable, but opted out of, in favor of another. It is also important to consider the opportunity cost of each option that could help you make a wise decision when there is a need to rebalance your portfolio. The formula you need to use is:

Opportunity Cost = Return of the First Option - Return of Selected Option

No matter what option you picked, the potential profit that you missed by not investing in that particular option is known as the opportunity cost.

For now, it is enough to know the basics. You will know more as you become more familiar with stock investing.

CHAPTER 3

How to Start Trading and What Do You Need Before You Start

Things to Consider Before Investing in A Stock

Plan the Investment

The first advice that we can give you about financial investments, is about planning of investments, understanding what the best actions are, and diversifying your portfolio.

Even if you have never experienced this chain of events firsthand, it is not a problem. Sooner or later you have to learn.

In order to better diversify your stock portfolio and understand where to invest, we recommend opening a demo account.

Plan Your Investment Strategies

Familiarize yourself with the platform.

Get familiar with the market.

If you decide to buy shares in an unconscious manner, and then open a real account and invest without the right measure, prepare to say goodbye to your capital. Of course, this is not the most appropriate and wise way to invest.

Draw the Investment Plan You Just Made

Writing an outline of your strategy will give you a firm base to start again in times of chaos, and will make you avoid making important investment decisions dictated by emotions.

It offers you a clear outline to review and change if, with time and experience, you notice defects or if you change your investment goals.

Learn the Difference Between Investing and Speculating

Understanding the difference between an investor and a speculator is very important. You need to know how to use the knowledge to your advantage, if you want to make the most out of your investments.

If you want to get the maximum profit in a short time, then you must have considerable minimum time to devote to the study of markets and financial instruments. You must understand the difference between speculator and investor.

Understand the Importance of Timing (And the Impossibility of Getting It Right)

It is very important to understand when the right time to buy and sell shares comes.

The timing is an indispensable part to identify the stocks to be bought.

If the correct price levels are not identified, there could very well be the risk of entering the market. This may be unfavorable, and may not allow us to accurately quantify the risk-return ratio of the transaction.

How to Invest in the Stock Market?

The stock market can definitely be your money-making machine if you do things right. But first, let me explain the procedure that is followed for making any investments in the stock market.

Determine Your Financial Goals

Before you put a single penny in stocks, you have to figure why you want to do this and what your investment goals are. You also have to perform an honest assessment of your current financial situation, so that you can be sure that you are in a place where you can accommodate this new activity.

Open a Retirement Account

If you are a beginner in stock market investing, then I would suggest that you start your journey by opening a retirement account, like the 401(k) or any other equivalent account. In case there is no employer plan, then you can also go with the Individual Retirement Account (IRA). These accounts are not only tax-sheltered, but they also allow you to invest your money in the stock market, until you are ready to do so directly.

Choose a Stockbroker

When you think you are ready to invest in the stock market on your own, the first thing to do is choose an online broker to suit your needs. Also, look at your budget because some of them may be giving you a lot of features, but they also charge hefty commissions. For starters, you have to understand that there are two types of stockbrokers: first there is the **full-service broker** whom carry out most of the work for their clients, their brokerage fee or commission is generally high; secondly there is the **discount Broker** whom focuses only in executing buying and selling orders for their clients.

Begin with Mutual Funds

I usually advise beginners to start investing in mutual funds, because you do not have to worry about anything with these funds. There are professional fund managers who will work on mitigating the risks, and also encourage good performance by implementing necessary strategies. You basically do not have to do any of those things, and the only thing that you have to do is figure out how much money you want to invest in these funds. One of the best things about mutual funds is that they are already diversified, so all your eggs are never in one basket.

Invest in Index Funds

If you want to make the process a bit more hassle-free, then I would suggest you start investing in index funds like the S&P 500 or Standard & Poor's 500 Index, which is a market-capitalization-weighted index of the 500 largest U.S. publicly traded companies. Other common U.S. stock market benchmarks include the Dow Jones Industrial Average or Dow 30 and the Russell 2000 Index, which represents the small-cap index.

Suppose you invest in an index fund that follows the S&P 500 ,the performance of your investment will follow it precisely. It is true that when you invest in an index fund, there are chances you will not over-perform. At the same time, there are chances you will not underperform as well.

Use Dollar-Cost Averaging Method

This is basically a process by which you get into any investment gradually rather than suddenly. For example, instead of investing an entire amount of $2000 in one index fund, you can invest say $200 investment every month for a period of ten months. By this process, you will never be buying at the top of the market, and instead, you buy at different times.

Educate Yourself About Investments

There is no end to how much you can learn about the stock market, and you should not ever stop learning. When you open an account with your broker, you are going to access to lots of resources on the platform itself. Even after that, you should look into different major financial magazines, buy books, and listen to podcasts, to develop trading psychology and know about all the latest strategies. You can also try paper trading, by which you will get the perfect opportunity to test your trading skills without losing any money. With time, you will be prepared to face the real world.

Go into Direct Stock Investments Gradually

Do you know why I asked you to open a retirement account, or start with mutual funds and index funds? It is because I want you to get yourself used to the market environment first. This is a gradual process. If you dive into the stock market right away, you probably do not know anything, and chances are that you will lose all your money. However, with gradual exposure, you will learn a thing or two every day and polish your skills in the process.

Monitor Your Portfolio

Once you start investing, you cannot simply put your money in one stock and never look at it. You have to monitor your portfolio constantly. You have to understand that the stock market is highly dynamic, and it will keep changing every minute. If you are not aware of what is going on, you may as well wake up one day, to find that all your capital is lost. But yes, I am not asking you to react to every rise or fall in price. Nevertheless, you should keep your research alive and wait patiently. If you notice any changes that might have a grave impact on your portfolio, you have to do some damage control.

Always Diversify!

If you have followed all the steps in the same order as I told you to, then your portfolio is already diversified by the time you reach the final step. Even after that, when you are investing in stocks directly, do not invest all your money in a single place. You should put some of your money in growth funds, some of it in bonds, and some in international funds. This will ensure that even if something happens in one of the funds, your money in other funds are safe.

CHAPTER 4

Techniques and Strategies That Will Help You

Value Investing

Value investors are shopping for stocks at a bargain with the intention of selling it at its value in the future. This strategy is founded upon the idea that there is a degree of irrationality in the market. This irrationality creates a scenario for value investors in which they can find stocks being sold at a discounted price. When these discounted stocks realize their value, the investor would then sell them off and earn through capital gain.

This strategy is based on the concept that investors should buy businesses and not the stock. All investment considerations are based on the state of the business/company. Stock market prices are just a gauge of how much an investor can potentially earn when the market realizes the real worth of a business.

Growth Investing

Growth investing involves looking at stocks owned by companies that have shown consistent growth and substantial profit in the past. Contrary to value investing, this strategy does not pay heed if the stock is trading above intrinsic value. In the eyes of the growth investor, the company has shown continued growth, and the intrinsic value would eventually follow, which makes the stock still a good investment.

Day trading

This method involves buying and selling a position within the same day. There are no leftover positions once the trading hours are over for the day. This helps traders limit their trading to stocks that can give them a reasonable return within the day. Also, it helps prevent losses on positions remaining at the end of the day.

This strategy requires a significant trading volume for each position to realize acceptable returns, while covering for any fees in the transactions.

Position Trading

This is a strategy that involves the trader holding a position longer than the average trader. It could last from a day up to a month, depending on the trend. Position traders enter a position when a trend has already been established. They only exit a position when it breaks the current trend.

Swing Trading

This is a strategy that takes advantage of the increased volatility when a new trend is starting. It is the middle ground between day trading and position trading, in terms of how long a position is held. Compared to the other strategies, it places a significant emphasis on fundamental analysis, since it is crucial that large-cap stocks are chosen. These stocks have a high trading volume, which would provide a greater potential return.

Scalping

This strategy takes advantage of the price gaps created by the bid-ask spreads on a stock. This is done by entering the bid price and exiting at the asking price. Scalpers trade in liquid markets to increase their trade frequency, since the strategy calls for taking advantage of small and frequent price movements. Furthermore, it works best in stocks that do not have sudden changes in market prices.

Index fund investing

This strategy is for the investors that do not have the time required for researching stocks that may be viable for investment. Index fund investing lets an investor passively participate in the returns of the stock market. Moreover, this strategy is the only way that an investor can guarantee their share of the returns experienced by the stock market. Unlike mutual fund investing, it does not involve the costs of mutual funds, such as advisory fees, portfolio transaction fees, and operating expenses.

You can do index fund investing by buying shares in index funds or ETFs tracking market indices. This will already provide you a diversified stock portfolio, while assuring that your portfolio reflects the return of the stock market. You can further diversify your stock holdings by investing in indices of a different markets, sectors, countries, or regions.

Dollar-cost Averaging

Dollar cost averaging is an investment strategy of making regular investments in the stock market. It can be used in combination with other investing strategies. The premise behind dollar cost averaging is that, fixed investments on a regular basis help investor avoid the temptation of timing the market. They are also purchasing in regular increments that result in a lower per-share cost. This method can be also be used in mutual funds and ETFs investing in the stock market.

Averaging down

This is an investment strategy where an investor purchases additional shares during downtrends. Like dollar-cost averaging, it can be used in conjunction with the other investment strategies. This works best in value investing, and stock dividend investing where the stocks are purchased with the long-term in mind. Even so, investors should be wary of averaging on downtrends that arise from the loss of book value, due to events or changes unaccounted for ,during your entry in the position.

CHAPTER 5

How Does Dividend Investing Works and How to Start with Profits and Risks

What Are Dividends?

In a simple way, a dividend is a payment made by the company to its investors out of its profits. Typically, dividends are paid out on a quarterly basis. The company is not required to pay dividends, and it is not required to use all of its profits to pay dividends. The amounts paid vary from company to company.

Most companies are seeking growth. Some are older and more established, and so they may not be seeking it in an aggressive fashion. Another factor that is important, is the industry that the company is involved in. Some companies are in highly competitive growth industries, such as technology companies. Think of Facebook, Apple, or Amazon. Others are slow-moving industries. Drug stores might be an example of this. There is still room for growth, but the growth is smaller and much slower, than the kind of a mover-and-shaker, like Amazon, is experiencing. Generally speaking, younger companies are going to see more rapid and aggressive growth than older companies.

Companies that are either in high growth industries or in a high growth phase, are going to want to invest more of their profits back into the company. These profits are going to be used for research and development, or expansion. They may build new plants, purchase new equipment, or hire more people. Those companies that are aggressively seeking growth are not going to be paying dividends.

When to Reinvest or Not to Reinvest

Remember, we discussed the two options to acquiring your dividend? You should consider it in this situation. It can be easier to choose to base on that, because you will know what your investment objectives are. Here, the simple thing you ought to do is taking the dividend in cash form. You now have the cash you can do whatever you want with. If you prefer passive income, so that you can withdraw the money from your trading account, this is the option you should go with.

Considering your age, this could be the best decision, as you will take advantage of compounding. On the other hand, reinvesting your dividends enables your shares to compound into more shares. Companies make it easy to do this through a feature called the **Dividend Reinvestment Plan (DRIP)**. DRIP automatically converts all your dividends paid into the shares without charging you a commission, and in some cases, you will get a 2-3% discount. To enroll in the DRIP program, simply consult your stockbroker. Not every stock has a DRIP; its existence depends on the decision of the company management.

How to Start Chasing Dividend Income

Pick a Type of Account

The first thing you need to do is pick a type of account you prefer to work with. Dividends are taxable in some countries, meaning you could benefit from keeping them in legally registered accounts like RRSP or TFSA. Deciding where to place your investments can be a very confusing thing. Below is what you need to take away from this subtopic:

TFSA: Applies to Canadian, American, and other international stocks and ETFs.

RRSP: Refers to Canadian, American, and other foreign stocks and ETFs.

Unregistered Accounts: Canadian, American, and other international stocks. Any margin trading engagements are also included. (They pay maximum taxes on dividends, and handle riskier investments to get capital investments, just in case an investment goes wrong.)

Generally, the fee charged on profits is lower than the one charged on a regular income. There are, however, many rules and exceptions, especially regarding US Stocks. It is hard to find a one-fits-all answer, and I would recommend you consult a professional, especially when your portfolio grows bigger.

Choose a Stockbroker

As you might know, the broker needs to provide the type of account you required in Step 1. You will also want a broker that offers a DRIP when chasing dividends. You should, therefore, be careful with the kind of broker you are opting for. Preferably, go for brokers that support registered accounts like RRSPs and TFSAs.

Decide between ETFs and Stocks

The essential dividend growth investing pertains to picking individual stocks using the metrics we discussed earlier in this article. There are plenty of ETFs in different countries that mainly focus on dividend income and have little management expenses. While ETFs charge a fee that digs into the returns, it is a shallow maintenance strategy. You do not need to look at individual companies and their payout ratios. Instead, what you need to focus on is the distribution you earn and the yield it provides you.

Keep on Contributing and Investing

This is a continuous process that does not stop once you purchase your first stocks. The case study we used above focused only on a one-time investment tracked over 20 years. You should, therefore, be making regular deposits and slowly be picking up even more ETFs and dividend stocks. This will result in your passive income stream growing at a faster rate. Ideally, you can use a DRIP, where possible, for most of your investment life to accelerate growth.

Creating Passive Income with Dividend Stocks

Dividend investing is one of the best ways to increase income through passive income. Living off the bonuses is not a sprint but a marathon. You should not, however, take the marathon lightly. You should have the urge to increase both your income and your retirements. Plant your precious dividend seed by investing in the dividend growth stocks. What will it need? Well, an average dividend yield of around 3% in your portfolio, you will need approximately a $3.33 million portfolio to earn $100,000 annually in dividend income.

The **annual dividend yield** refers to the calculation of the general percentage of a dividend per share in received in relation to the stock price. It is a good barometer of the annual income earned from investing in a stock. For example, if you invest in a $100 stock, and it pays $2 per share in dividends. This is equal to a 4% dividend yield a year.

It is not possible to start living off your dividends right away after investing, but it can happen over some time. But with a good plan and strategy, you can achieve the goal of passive income and living off dividends sooner than you imagine. The key to living off dividends is focusing on dividend growth stocks. The dividend growth stocks increase annually, which increases your income without you doing a single thing! Remember when I talked about planting a seed? Well, if you invest the right way, your seed will grow into a huge redwood tree!

How to Generate a Passive Income Annually from Dividend Stocks

So, how do you generate a passive income each year from dividend stocks? When you are building a dividend portfolio, start scaling smaller positions that you will continue to develop over sometime. First, use a brokerage that gives the lowest commission fee on trading. They are brokers that allow you to trade completely commission-free on all the stocks and options. This is a very lucrative deal because options are usually essential to purchase. When properly used, options are an excellent way to mitigate risk in your account or portfolio. These are the best stocks when it comes to covered call writing.

Track Record

While the past performances might not be the best guide to the future, companies that have the unquestionable capability of delivering profits over a long period may be economic moats. For instance, they may have a stronger brand and lower costs. This suggests that their future dividend growth will be robust and resilient. This can be better if that company has a history of rewarding its shareholders by paying out dividends with profit gains.

Management Focus

Through reading and analyzing a company's annual report, you can be able to ascertain management standpoints in the future dividend growth. For instance, several management teams will pay attention to the reinvestment of excess capital to enhance future sales and the profitability of the business.

Company Type

While different industries like technology might offer more earnings growth ratio, they are doubtful to give generous dividend growth due to massive investments of capital. Similarly, a less mature business may need more significant investments and might be unable to pay out dividends to the shareholders. Therefore, it can be prudent for an investor to carefully assess the maturity of the business as well as its sector stability, before purchasing. For the investors seeking more than just a passive income, mature stocks in more established industries could be the right place to start when choosing the best income opportunities.

Diversification

As much as a lot of investors prefer to majorly focus on the potential return from investing their funds in the stock market, learning how to reduce the risk could be the most sensible starting point. After all, you can gain from getting a passive income in a short period, only for the dividend income to be hit by huge losses further down the line. Therefore, looking to reduce a company risk could be a worthy move. This is the danger posed by difficulties encountered by businesses that can lead to a decline in the stock price. In portfolios that have a small number of stocks, the company-specific risk will be extremely high due to a decline in a single stock, resulting in major loses for the general collection.

High Yields

As much as it might be obvious that buying high-yield stocks is an excellent means of making a monthly passive income, it is nevertheless the quickest method of achieving that goal. When determining which stocks the investor might be interested in, it could be worth working in reverse. What this means is, first find out how much income you need in a single month. Secondly, consider the average yield you need from your portfolio to hit the target. This way, you will be in a better position to exclude those stocks that give low dividend returns that are unable to provide your preferred level of monthly income.

Long-Term Hold

With the increasing number of stocks available to investors in different sectors and countries, it is very tempting to keep switching from one capital to the other, depending on the current state of things in the economy. In terms of being the best way to use your funds, this may seem like the best idea at the time, but the harsh truth is that buying and selling regularly can result in inflated dealing costs. Similarly, it may also mean that stocks kept in a portfolio are not given the time they need to be profitable. Therefore, holding dividend stocks over a prolonged period of time could be the best method of generating a passive income. This means the investor will only use little effort, yet still have a good chance of potentially higher returns.

CHAPTER 6

How to Set Your Portfolio

The Most Effective Method to Fabricate A Wise Investment Portfolio

Enhancement is the way to progress when investing. In general, spreading your money around diminishes risk by guaranteeing your portfolio's exhibition is not excessively reliant on any one specific resource.

In any case, expansion does not mean you need to step into extraordinary resources. Rather, we prescribe utilizing minimal-effort, listed funds (mutual funds or ETFs) for the main part of your portfolio investments. That is because these funds track wide indexes (for example, the S&P 500), and offer a simple method to accomplish that exceedingly significant enhancement inexpensively.

Broadening additionally implies investing in various resources that are not profoundly connected, which means they do not move in lockstep. Stocks and bonds have had a negative relationship since the 1990s. When stock costs have gone up in the past, bond costs have gone down, and vice versa.

You may have heard proposals about how a lot of cash to assign to stocks versus bonds. General guidelines propose subtracting your age from 100 or 110 to choose how your portfolio ought to be invested. In case you are 30 years old, these principles recommend 70-80% of your portfolio distributed to stocks and 20%-30% of your portfolio to bonds. In your 60s, that the proposed proportions are 40%-50% assigned to bonds, and 50-60% to stocks.

Despite everything, some investors like the general guideline; yet others see it as too shortsighted because it disregards your risk appetite. Whatever blend of stocks and securities you choose for your portfolio, such expansion can be accomplished utilizing the ease file funds referenced previously. You do not have to delve into the universe of individual stocks or bonds, if you prefer not to.

Lastly, if this feels like more than you need to choose, a portfolio the executive's administration, called a 'robot-advisor', would settle on all these designation choices for you. After you answer a couple of inquiries concerning your investment objectives and risk resilience, these mechanized investing administrations will construct and deal in your portfolio for a minimal effort.

Have A Ton of Fun with Your Portfolio

A few people are content with a 'set-it-and overlook-it' investing procedure, while others favor a hands-on approach. In any case, I prescribe organizing minimal effort record funds for the lion's share of your investment portfolio. Indeed, even proficient investors who pick stocks professionally frequently utilize these funds for their own investments.

However, if you intend to commit a great deal of time following the market, I prescribe that you keep progressively risky wagers (trading stocks, options, future, or others) close to 10% of your portfolio's value. Why? Once more, you need to secure your savings, on the off chance that a definite wager ends up being a failure.

Building an Investment Portfolio

As an investor, the best approach is diversification. **Diversification** means investing your funds in different securities. This is highly advisable because of the inherent and underlying risks posed by the markets. It is a fact that the price or value of stocks keeps changing almost all the time. Putting all your eggs in one basket is a risky affair, just in case things go wrong. Diversification means no matter what happens, you can still be profitable.

Principles of Building A Portfolio

We can define portfolio management as an approach of balancing rewards and risks. In order to meet your investment goals, you will need to invest in a wide variety of products including SMAs, REITs, close-ended funds, ETFs and others. It is a very good idea and is highly recommended to have an investment plan. Determine what your end goal is, especially when there are numerous options available.

Portfolio management often means different things to different investors. Think about a young person fresh from college and on his first job. Such a person views portfolio management as a way of growing investments and providing a pretty decent amount over time for future use. On the other hand, a relatively older person, who has either been working or been in business for a time, will view things differently.

Such a person will view portfolio management as an excellent chance of holding on to their wealth accumulated possibly over the years. There are different ways of organizing and planning portfolio management. A portfolio manager should be able to handle the various needs that different investors have, when coming up with a diversified portfolio. This is why individualized approach is the highly advised option. Here are some basic principles of developing a portfolio.

First, it is advisable to note the availability of numerous options. This means that there are plenty of investment vehicles to choose from. Therefore, a client or investor needs to determine their goals: whether they wish to create wealth over time; whether they want to put away funds for future use, whether they want to generate a regular income, and so on. This way, it will be possible to come up with a suitable investment plan. Such a plan should incorporate appetite for risk, time period, and similar aspects.

How to Build a Portfolio of Stocks to Invest in

Your portfolio must be able to sustain your future capital needs and give you peace of mind. As an investor, you can design a portfolio according to your goals and strategies. The following are some of the things that can help you build your stocks portfolio.

Determine the Asset Allocation That You Think Is Suitable for You

It is important to ascertain your investment goals and financial situation first, before you decide to create a portfolio. You need to consider the following: your age; amount of investment capital; duration of investment for growth; future capital needs; and your investment philosophy. A young man or woman, who is just starting his or her career, requires a different investment strategy, as compared to a 50-year-old mother looking for ways to help her child graduate from college, and to live in comfort when she retires.

Create Your Portfolio According to Your Design

When you are certain about the asset allocation that you want, you can now proceed with dividing your capital according to the set allocations of your chosen profile.

The different asset classes can be split into subclasses, which offer different potential returns and risks. You can divide your allocation for stock between different market caps and sectors, as well as foreign and domestic stocks. You can also divide your allocation towards bonds.

Rebalance Your Portfolio

There is a need to periodically analyze and rebalance your portfolio because your initial proportions may be affected by the market movements. You must quantitatively classify the investments and verify the proportion of their worth to the whole, when you need to assess the actual asset allocation of your portfolio.

Things like risk tolerance, future needs, and financial situation may likely change over time. In case these things change, you may need to make necessary adjustments to your portfolio.

CHAPTER 7

How to Evaluate and Compare Stocks

Various Types of Stocks

Essentially, there are two kinds of stock issues. There are common stock shares and preferred stock shares.

Common Stock Shares

Common (ordinary) stock shares are, well, the most widely recognized when alluding to buying and selling stocks. The share offers ownership in the organization, and voting rights to help toward the administration of the organization. The common stock offers returns through capital growth.

Preferred Stocks

Preferred stock shares, much like corporate security, do not offer any voting rights. Be that as it may, preferred stock ordinarily offers stable dividends, not at all like regular stock where the profit can be variable, pulled back or not at all. Another insurance that is offered to preferred stock owners is they are paid before regular stockholders on account of the liquidation of the organization.

Custom Stock Classes

Preferred and common stock are two significant styles of stock. It is likewise feasible for companies to redo various classes of stock to fit the necessities of their investors. The reason for making classes of shares is so the organization can retain control inside a specific gathering of proprietors. These various classes are frequently assigned in their trading images by including the letter A or B at the end of the image.

Warrant Stocks

Also, a few stocks are sold and put under warrant. A warrant regularly is set on insiders or starting investors that claim over 10% of the organization's shares. The warrant normally expresses that the shares cannot be sold for 3 to 5 years. Different sorts of warrants permit the insiders to buy more stock after a given time.

To summarize everything, most stocks are given as common. Common stock can get variable dividends and have voting rights. Preferred stock ordinarily costs more to buy, yet have a profit fixed with higher bank rights than the common shareholder. Both face the risk of organization disappointment.

What Determines Stock Price?

When the first sale of stock has finished, the stock cost can move autonomously for the real organization's prosperity; a current model is the out of this world stock cost for Tesla (ticker: TSLA), an organization that might be a long time from profitability.

Things being what they are, what causes stock prices to go up or down? The basic answer is the organic market. Value changes reflect market interest. Prices go up when a stock is considered alluring because of latest accomplishments of an organization, belongs to a company in a solid industry division, or is robust and well-known. On the off chance that investors are reluctant to buy a stock because of weak performance, a feeble industry, or being overpriced, that absence of interest will make value drop. Sooner or later, the cost will move low enough that investors are again ready to buy, and the cycle will start from the very beginning once more. Value investors, like Warren Buffett, represent considerable authority in finding disagreeable stocks in overlooked enterprises that, despite everything, have solid earnings and a strong future. They buy them (or buy the whole organization, as Buffett frequently does) and trust that the price will rise.

CHAPTER 8

Beginners' Mistakes That Should Be Avoided

Poor Preparation: "If you fail to plan, then you are planning to fail" cit

If you are on the edge on buying now and ask later , well that may cause you to blow your account. In Day Trading we use "FOMO" which stand for "Fear Of Missing Out". When you see that the stock is going well and you don't want to miss out the opportunity so you buy it, it can easily go sideways and the stock can drop the next minute. If you are an investor, you need to know the stocks viable for your investment strategy (and have a strategy in the first place!) before you buy it.

Wake up few hours before the market opens and start to study how the stocks are moving. Plan your losses , because is when you know what you are likely to lose, that you can control them.

Trading is 90% planning and 10% execution when the market is open.

Being Emotional

Greed, hope, and fear have no place in your decisions in the stock market. As new traders tend to check their P&L (profit and loss report) of the day and forget to follow the plan. You may start to have a really good earning and decide to keep going on buying and selling with no break. Let's say you are starting to lose which will make you emotional ,leading you to revenge trading as you will try to get back what you lost ,maybe from the same stock with no plan. Huge Mistake!

When you feel distressed or emotional it's time to shut down the computer. Walk away from it as emotional trading will take home bigger losses.

Anticipating Returns and scaling up your shares size to quick

If you are anticipating potential returns, you are closing yourself off to the possibility that your stock positions could turn against you. This is a dangerous mindset to have, since the conditions of a stock or the market can change. If this change occurs, whatever you know before is already inaccurate, and you need to adjust. This adjustment is hard to do, if you set your mind up to think your returns are already realized.

If you are ready to lose $50 in order to gain $100 and you decide to scale up quickly to gain more profit , you have to take in consideration the increase of your losses. Not doing so will lead to emotional trading and you may lose your account as not ready to play hard.

Scale slow and prepare yourself mentally to the losses that you will have on doing so.

Dependence on Tools

The tools are there to help you make better decisions. However, these tools cannot analyze the data and make the decisions for you. You still need to think whether what these tools are telling you is actually relevant. They are not exempt from having limitations on how to help you. You need to understand the different tools available to you and only use these in the right situations.

Spend time on "paper trading" apps , be responsible with the fake money as they were yours so that you can learn faster. If you are planning to open an account with $5000,00 don't start with a $50000.00 in fake account ,as you won't understand how to manage the smaller amount.

CHAPTER 9

What Is Meant By Day Trading And How It Operates

What Is Day trading?

Day trading is done on different platforms and systems, and the operator must be familiar with the trade. Learn to study the basic movements and keep an eye on technological developments over time.

Most traders lose daily transactions. In general, they most often lose some money. It is also essential to focus and rationale for a period of losses and does not let the fundamental fact that the monetary value also lost. Focus on the future activities of daily transactions by implementing some of the strategies outlined in the grand scheme.

Independence is to build your own set of tools. The patience is key for the day trader. Plan and analyze the market , come up with a strategy after observing the market and its ups and downs.

Getting stuck in the past, makes many prisoners. Provident allowed to see the possible moves, and gives a final air for future business activities will consider the requirements of a day trader. The trader continues to follow his vision, which implies clear mental processing about their next possible moves after careful consideration. This accelerates trading, simplifies future daily operations and the chances are that you will succeed.

Day traders do not need to be tycoons, but they must have a specific amount of money that has been specially selected to start the trading day. I remember the first days are always a win-or-lose situation, but you continue to learn and grow. This money can be lost as well. Be careful when handling your finances in day trading. Not every story is a good story.

High interest in something is the objective to hold successfully. Experience comes with a lot of falling and learning. You get exposure to various sources of learning and controlling cost in every movement during the trading day, to squeeze the best. Getting real experience and knowledge of multiple platforms of negotiation and the strategies needed to succeed to make trading worth it.

How Day trading Works

Once you start day trading, you can use a myriad number of techniques and methods to execute trades. For example, either you can choose to trade based solely on your gut feeling, or you can go to the other extreme of relying entirely on mathematical models that optimize trading success through elaborate automated trading systems.

Regardless of the method, you can have limitless day-trading profit potential once you master day trading. Here are some of the strategies many expert day traders use profitably.

One is called **'trading the news'**, which is one of the most popular day trading strategies since time immemorial. As you may have already gleaned from the name, it involves acting upon any press-released information such as economic data, interest rates, and corporate earnings.

Another popular day trading strategy is called **'fading the gap at the open'**. This one is applicable on trading days when the price of a security opens with a gap, i.e., either below the previous day's lowest price or above the previous day's highest price.

'Fading the gap at the open' means taking an opposite position from the gap's direction. If the price opens with a downward gap, i.e., below the previous day's lowest price, you buy the security. If the price opens with an upward gap, i.e., it opens higher than the previous day's highest price, you short or sell the security.

There was a time when the only people able to trade in financial markets were those working for trading houses, brokerages, and financial institutions. The rise of the internet, however, made things easier for individual traders to get in on the action. Day trading, in particular, can be a very profitable career, as long as one goes about it in the right way.

However, it can be quite challenging for new traders, especially those who lack a good strategy. Furthermore, even the most experienced day traders hit rough patches occasionally. As stated earlier, day trading is the purchase and sale of an asset within a single trading day. It can happen in any marketplace, but it is more common in the stock and forex markets.

Day traders use short-term trading strategies and a high level of leverage to take advantage of small price movements in highly liquid currencies or stocks. Experienced day traders have their fingers on events that lead to short-term price movements, such as the news, corporate earnings, economic statistics, and interest rates, which are subject to market psychology and market expectations.

When the market rises or falls to meet those expectations, it causes unexpected, significant moves that can benefit attuned day traders. However, venturing into this line of business is not a decision prospective day trader should take lightly. It is possible for day traders to make a comfortable living trading for a few hours each day.

However, for new traders, this kind of success takes time. Think like several months or more than a year. For most day traders, the first year is quite tough. It is full of numerous wins and losses, which can stretch anyone's nerves to the limit. Therefore, a day trader's first realistic goal should be to hold on to his/her trading capital.

Volatility is the name of the game when it comes to day trading. Traders rely on a market or stock's fluctuations to make money. They prefer stocks that bounce around several times a day, but do not care about the reason for those price fluctuations. Day traders will also go for stocks with high liquidity, which will allow them to enter and exit positions without affecting the price of the stock.

Day traders might short sell a stock if its price is decreasing, or purchase if it is increasing. Actually, they might trade it several times in a day, purchasing it and short selling it a number of times, based on the changing market sentiment. In spite of the trading strategy used, their wish is for the stock price to move.

Day trading, however, is tricky for two main reasons. Firstly, day traders often compete with professionals, and secondly, they tend to have psychological biases that complicate the trading process.

Professional day traders understand the traps and tricks of this form of trading. In addition, they leverage personal connections, trading data subscriptions, and state-of-the-art technology to succeed. However, they still make losing trades. Some of these professionals are high-frequency traders whose aim is to skim pennies off every trade.

The day trading field is a crowded playground, which is why professional day traders love the participation of inexperienced traders. Essentially, it helps them make more money. In addition, retail traders tend to hold on to losing trades too long and sell winning trades too early.

Due to the urge to close a profitable trade to make some money, retail investors sort of pick the flowers and water the weeds. In other words, they have a strong aversion to make even a small loss. This tends to tie their hands behind their backs when it comes to purchasing a declining asset. This is due to the fear that it might decline further.

CHAPTER 10

The Meaning And Importance of Volume, Price, And Technical Indicators

How Is Stock Price Determined?

Now that we have covered the basics about the stock market, it is time we look into some of the finer details like how the stock prices are determined. Stock prices go up and down all the time, but do you know why? If you want to pinpoint the exact reason behind the price of a stock, then I am telling you this right now – it is impossible. There is not one, but many factors acting behind the price of a single stock, and it is not influenced singularly by any of them. But yes, with a little effort, you can easily understand the basics behind the price determination of stocks.

Before that, let me give you a brief introduction to capital markets. **Primary markets** are set up so that a company can raise money through an initial public offering (IPO). An initial price is set up after consulting the investment bankers, and then investors start lining up for the stocks of that company.

When the IPO is done, the stocks are bought by the common investors who can then, in turn, buy or sell them in the **secondary market**. This happens in different stock exchanges. Now, here the price is influenced by demand and supply. The ultimate price of the shares will be decided by the bid and ask price. The **ask price** is referred to as the minimum price that the seller will accept to get the concerned security. The **bid price** is the highest price that the buyers are ready to pay for purchasing the concerned shares.

Some other factors that are important when you are discussing the price or when the price is determined, are as follows.

The first factor is the earnings of the company in question. I will agree that the stock price is definitely not influenced on a daily basis by this factor, but before any investment decisions are finalized, the earnings of the company are something that will be looked into by analysts.

Institutional investors and the trades they perform, is the second factor that you should have a look at. Hedge funds, mutual funds, or even pension plans might be included in this.

Thirdly, good or bad market events can directly influence the price of the stocks as well. For example, in 2008, everyone remember the financial crisis where the S&P500 stocks, crushed down to a 38% loss.

Technical Indicators

A **technical indicator** is a pattern you see in price levels, which are designed to help you predict the future price. There are various indicators, such as candlestick patterns, Relative Strength Index, MACD, Money Flow Index, stochastics, and Bollinger bands. Sounds complicated, right?

There are definitely some technical indicators that are more difficult to learn. We will not focus on those in this beginner's guide. The only technical indicator that will be explained is the support and resistance pattern.

CHAPTER 11

Risk and Account Management in Day Trading

Risk Management

Investing in the stock market can be a very risky business. While there are some risks that you can control, there are also those that you cannot and thus you can only guard against. Investors are only able to keep their stocks and bonds at acceptable risk levels, by having investment selections thoughtful enough to meet their goals. However, there are some risks that are inherent to investing and traders have no control over such risks. Most of the risks that investors have no control over, affect the stock market or the economy at large. Thus, the only thing traders can do is adjust their portfolios, otherwise quit the business. Some of the risks that every investor is likely to face are discussed below.

Risk in the stock market is caused by interest rates, equity prices, foreign exchange rates, and commodity prices. A higher interest rate makes it more expensive to borrow money for both businesses and consumers, slowing down economic activity. Bonds are also affected by the prevailing interest rate in an economy, but in the inverse direction. Higher interest rates drive down demand for bonds, and cause an overall lag in the trading volumes of the stock market. As for stocks, the interest rate affects not just the performance of listed companies; it influences the ability of the public and brokerage firms to deal in leveraged stock purchases. A higher interest rate, therefore, spells doom for the whole stock market.

Price risk comes from the volatility of stocks. It is the probability that the price of a stock or stocks in an investment portfolio will fall over a long period of time. The risk of a stock dropping in price can either be systematic or unsystematic. **Systematic risk** is the risk that occurs across the whole stock market, bringing down the price of stocks in many or all sectors of the economy. **Unsystematic risk**, on the other hand, affects a single stock or the stocks in a particular industry, like the oil and gas sector when oil prices drop.

Assessing Your Risk Tolerance

Each one of us has a different level of risk tolerance. To assess your risk tolerance, answer the following question. What are my goals?

Investing is most effective when you have a perfect idea of what you are accumulating money for. It is even better when you have a solid idea of exactly how much money you are going to need, or at least a fairly accurate estimate. Based on goals alone, the more the money you need to attain a particular goal, the lesser the risk tolerance you can withstand, because it is better to have a fraction of the money you need to achieve a certain goal than lose all your money. With a properly formulated investment strategy and a well-defined tolerance for risk, you can proceed to invest prudently, and hopefully make enough money to meet your goals.

The Dangers of Ignoring Risk Tolerance

Before investing, it is very important that you determine your risk tolerance. Not only should you determine how much risk you can stand, but you should also make sure that you have it written down somewhere you are not likely to forget. When you start investing, every investment should be confined to within the safest bounds of your risk tolerance. You can lose your money on nearly every kind of investment, but the levels of risk vary from one asset to another and from stock to stock. When you do not factor in your risk tolerance, you are likely to panic and exit from an investment when it is within your risk levels, and possibly lose money.

Volatility Risks

Volatility risk is also referred to as involuntary or **market risk**. Volatility refers to the price fluctuations of a portfolio or security occurring over one year. In the stock market, all securities are subjected to market risks and this also includes events that are beyond an investor's control. Such events not only affect a single company or industry, but also affect the market and economy at large.

Geopolitical Events

Today, the world has become more globalized than ever. Economies continue to be connected at a very high rate. In this era of globalized economies, if say there is a recession in India, then the impact of this recession can also affect the economy of China. Furthermore, a geopolitical event like the withdrawal of a member state from the European Union could spark trade war among these member countries, and the end impact would be very devastating on individual economies around the world.

Economic Events

Economic events can include monetary policies, changes in interest rates, unforeseen deregulation or regulations, the effects of weather on the gross domestic product (GDP) of a country, tax revisions and relations between countries. All these are factors that greatly affect businesses and companies thus affecting the stock market.

Inflation

Inflation is also referred to as the purchasing power risk. Inflation simply refers to the reduction of the future value of assets or income as a result of the rising costs of goods and services. Inflation can also be a deliberate action by the government of a country. In volatility, the price fluctuations over some time are not indicated in the direction of a price movement (upward or downward movements). Volatility is expressed as *beta*. Volatility reflects the correlation between the price of a security and the stock market as a whole.

Strategies for Managing Volatility

Here are the strategies that you can adopt to reduce the impact of volatility.

Always invest in stocks whose dividends rise Consistently

Try to reduce exposure to high volatility securities. Assess your portfolio; try to eliminate or reduce high-volatility securities, as this is the most effective way to lower overall market risk.

Timing Risks

Market pundits will claim that the key to be successful in the stock market is buying low and selling high. Although this is good advice, the only factor making it be challenging is that it is very hard to implement it, due to the constant changes in prices. If you have been investing for a time, probably you have experienced the frustrations that come with buying at the highest price, beat it in a day, a week or a quarter. This is also similar to the experiences of trying to sell a stock at its lowest value.

Dollar-Cost Averaging

As an investor, you can reduce timing risks by buying or selling a fixed percentage of your portfolio holding/security. This plan is also referred to as the **constant dollar plan**. With this plan, you will have more shares being purchased even when the price of the stock is low. This, therefore, reduces your risk of buying at the top or even selling at the bottom.

CHAPTER 12

Examples of Day Trades, Advice and Methods That Beginners Should Know

Profitable Stocks for the Best Investor

Each month, we see thousands of people on Internet search engines search for topics such as "best stocks to buy today" or "2020 top stocks," or "the stocks to buy". Their appeal is understandable. However, the underlying fact is that most of the articles that will pop up first are those that are often written by freelancers who have never even tried investing in the stocks. These freelancers are just writing for page views and not doing serious research that provides readers with value as well as long-term relationships. You have been able to go through the topics covered above and one truth remains: investing is not a kid's play, such that you will grow to be an expert just after few hours or days of doing it. Investing is hard, and building an effective portfolio consisting of top stocks is something that cannot be done with perfection even by financial professionals. As observed, after fees, approximately 15% of actively managed funds can outperform the S&P 500 and this comes after a long period. This is even worse for the average non-professional investor, because it's very hard to beat inflation. In most cases, an average investor underperforms the S&P 500

84.23% OF FUNDS UNDERPERFORMED THE S&P 500®

15.77% OF FUNDS OUTPERFORMED THE S&P 500®

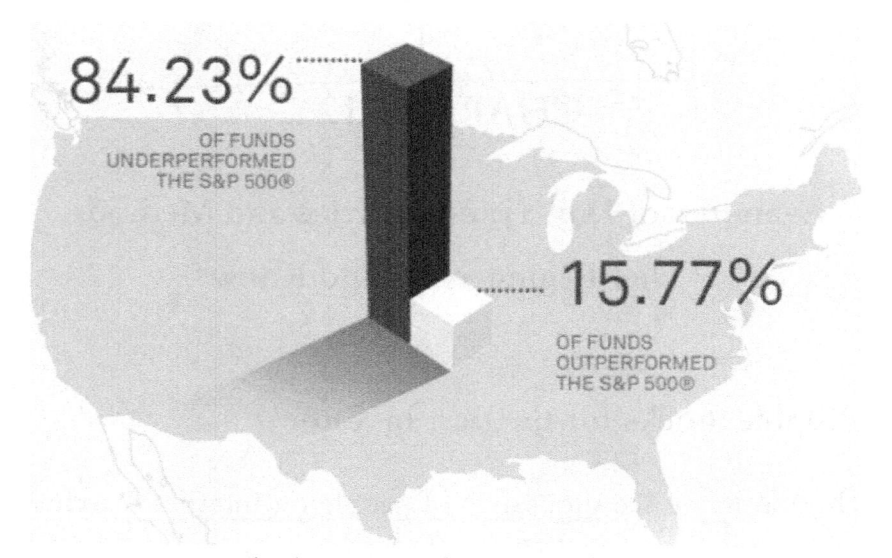

Figure 1: Funds that outperformed and underperformed the S&P 500 (Source: S&P 500 SPIVA)

The main reason as to why average investors underperform the S&P 500 is that most of these investors have developed the tendency of buying stocks or funds when market tops, and in this time, funds and stocks are expensive. However, after purchasing high, they then make a mistake of selling their funds and stocks right after a crash, and at this time, they are usually very cheap. This is what they keep doing over the years and the returns are discouraging.

On the other hand, genius investors who invest in value, like Warren Buffett, focus on building money during rhapsodic bull markets ,because at such a time, everything is expensive and only a few stocks can meet the strict investment criteria of bull markets. Therefore, eventually, when there is a stock market crash, only the top stocks are on sale everywhere. Thus, this enables investors, like Warren, to deploy their cash hoard, making them a bargain for decades to come. However, in as much as this approach appears to be simple, it is not easy and calls for a lot of discipline and focus. It also requires that you buy stocks of high-performing companies that are usually sold at consistent and reasonable prices.

Dividend Growth Investing: Case Study

In this case, we make up a situation to show you just how great dividend growth investing can be. Let us assume you bought $10,000 worth of Toyota shares on the New York Stock Exchange in early 1999. Below is how much you will have at the moment. A total of 243 shares of Toyota, worth $41.02 each, translates to $4,296.34 in passive income in the next 12 months ($1.22 per share annually), with 2.96% dividend yield ($296.45/$10,000). Fast forward to 2019; you made five times your initial investment mainly due to capital gains. Interestingly, your passive income grew even more, multiplying itself more than seven times the initial amount. The outcome (passive income growth) was due to two factors: **dividend reinvestments** and **dividend pay raise**.

Investment Criteria for Top Stocks

Although it is hard to outperform markets as an investor, individual stocks can be a very valuable component in your portfolio. We have discussed before that the most important thing as an investor is to find the right investment strategy that fits your goals and personality. Although your interest is in having a strategy that performs well, just ensure that it is a strategy that you are comfortable with and will always give you the interest to regularly invest.

It is appropriate that an investor, have some index funds. Investing in dividend growth can be a very good strategy if you look forward on doing that for a longer time, like 10 years or above. This is an effective strategy that can provide you with a reliable investment income even higher than index funds, thus allowing you as an investor to run about a variety of businesses.

Therefore, you can choose to buy shares of companies. Your shares will produce cash dividends and one thing is that these dividends grow each year. Depending on your needs and goals, you can choose to reinvest these dividends into buying more shares. Rather than spending more time predicting and hoping that stock prices will move up and not down, you can choose to be a dividend investor. As a dividend investor, your focus will be on the underlying fundamental factors behind the growth and safety of a company's dividends. You can also watch and analyze a company's strong long-term performance. Focusing on a company's performance provides a clear view than just focusing on the daily fluctuations of stock prices, and this is what will help you build good investment fundamentals. Below are the criteria for selecting top stocks to invest in:

- Check if the company maintains a strong balance sheet and historical performance, especially during recessions.
- Check if the company's risk of obsolescence is little and foreseeable. Also, ensure that this company is a beneficiary of long-term trends.

- Check if the returns on invested capital are above average. If so, check if it has a durable economic moat, that will keep it that way.
- Check if the company is a premium provider. What do they base their belief on? Is it quality or just price? It is preferred that companies that compete over quality are the best.
- Check if the tenure of the management team of a company. Long tenures suggest that the company focuses on long-term results.
- Check if the company is in your portfolio to understand it better.

How to Succeed in the Stock Market?

If you want to be a successful investor, you have to understand that there is no shortcut to that – you simply have to put in more effort. If you are someone who is following the feelings that your gut tells you, that is not how you can be successful. In fact, that is how you are going to lose a lot of money. If you had guessed something and it turned out to be right, then you cannot call that a win. It was simply a coincidence. In order to succeed, you have to design full-proof strategies and also execute them in the right manner. Just like in a game of football, the team does not enter the field without a strategy; similarly, if you want to win in the stock market, do not set foot if you have not devised your strategy yet.

CHAPTER 13

How to Buy Your First Stock

Picking Out Stocks to Invest In

Pick A Sector That Is Doing Well

When you are picking out stocks, it is important that you find some that come from a business sector that is also doing well. Depending on how the economy is doing, it is possible that some industries will still do well in a downturn, or at least some industries will do better than the rest. There are also times when the economy is doing well, but one or two industries are not doing as well as the rest of the market.

Growing Profits

You also need to look for a company that is making profits. If you see a company that is losing money from the start, then it will be hard for you to get a good return on investment. You also want to make sure that the company is getting bigger profits each year. When the company keeps on growing their profits, it is doing well and has a lot of popularity that is growing as well. This makes it a good investment option for many people. The bigger the profits, the better return on investment you will be able to get.

The Size of Your Company

Some investors want to work with a company that is a little bit smaller. They think that these are easier to work with, and that they will be able to monitor that company a little bit better than some of the bigger companies. However, there have been some studies done that show how smaller companies will actually carry more risks with them, compared to investing in some of the bigger companies.

Look at The Dividend Payments

When you look at a company, check and see if they are able to pay out dividends to their investors. Companies that are able to share their profits are great options for a beginner to work with. This shows that the company is already able to manage their debts, while still sharing the profits with the shareholders. It is likely that they will be able to do it again and you will continue to receive these payments in the future.

Manageable Debt

While you are taking a look at some of these companies to invest in, you should take a look at the debts that they have. The company does not necessarily need to be completely debt free, but they need to have a good balance between the amount of debt that they take on and the amount of profit that they are able to bring out.

Go with Liquid Stocks

Try to find a stock that has a happy medium. You want it to be at a good price, so you do not want the demand for that stock to be too high. If the demand is too high, it will be too expensive to get a hold of it to start. However, the demand needs to be high enough that when you are ready to leave the market, no matter what the reason is, you will be able to find someone who is willing to purchase the stocks from you.

Buying Your First Stock

When the time comes to prepare and make your first trade, you need to consider how you are going to purchase stocks, based on the trading plan you created in the previous chapter. Only by ensuring these things are in order, will you be able to get started with the odds in your favor.

Finding A Brokerage

The most common way to go about investing in stocks is through a brokerage. As the name implies, a **brokerage** tasks a broker to deal with sellers and buyers, while at the same time charging a fee for their services, and sometimes taking a commission from the profits as well. There are two common types of brokerages: those that offer a variety of additional services, including trading advice; and those that are more bare bones in comparison. If you are interested in putting in a minimum amount of work required for a successful return on your investment, then you may be interested in a full-service brokerage that will do most of the work for you. Alternately, you can choose an online brokerage that is little more than a platform, for you to trade however you please.

Research Stocks

Sticking to one type of stock, to start, will make it much easier for you to find the best stocks that are right for your plan. In order to invest in a stock with confidence, it is crucial that you have taken the time to understand exactly what it is that you are getting yourself into.

Buying Your First Stock

After you have done your research and found a few stocks that align with your goals as well your plan, it is time to get ready to actually complete your first trade. This can be more complicated than you might expect. However, which is why this section will break down the concepts you will come across when placing your trades. First and foremost, it is important to keep in mind that 'executing a trade' refers to the specific transaction; while using the term 'trade' in other contexts can refer to the type of trading plan or strategy you are using as well.

Depending on the current state of the stock you are considering to purchase, in addition to the direction where the research you have done is pointing to, not to mention the strength of the market as a whole, you will either want to buy (go long on) or sell (go short on) the stock in question. When placing a trade via a brokerage platform, that trade then goes out via their network and connects you with another individual who is interested in completing your requested transaction. Depending on the type of brokerage you are working with, you may also find they have shares of the requested stock available as well. Either way, just expect to pay fees as well as a commission to the brokerage and make sure that you factor these fees into your trading plan as well.

Regardless of the types of trades you want to complete, you will also be dealing with one or more of the following types of orders.

Market Order

This is a request that you send that sets off the transaction that will result in the buying or selling of a stock. You do not have much control over this request as the market is going to dictate the price you can expect in the transaction.

Limit Order

If, based on your research, you like the look of the direction the stock in question is moving, you can set a limit order which says you will buy or sell when the price reaches a certain level specifically. This helps to negate the issue of volatility.

Stop Order

This is the request to sell off all of your shares of a specific stock if the price hits a precise target. This should be set for every trade at a point just above when holding onto the stock becomes unfavorable.

Stop Limit Order

This is a combination of the above, and it keeps all aspects of a given stock price movement under close watch for specific triggers.

Trailing Stop Order

This is more versatile than a standard stop, and will only trigger if the price falls to a specific amount of a preset total, as opposed to when it reaches a given price. If you are looking to make truly long-term investments, then these will be your best choice as you can set them based on your overall level of risk assessment.

CHAPTER 14

How to Generate Passive Income in The Stock Market

How to Make Money in the Stock Market

While buying your first stock can be exciting, if you want to make money as a trader, you have to sell the stock. Here, the general rule of thumb is to buy low and sell high. While I mentioned above that buying at the right time increases the possibility of turning a profit, selling at the right time guarantees you that profit. If you sell at the wrong time, any advantages you had from buying at the right time are negated.

Selling your stocks can be a very emotionally-charged affair. Even if you have already made a profit, deciding whether to take those profits, or hold on to the stock in the hope that it will rise even higher, can be a difficult call. If your position is already in loss, it can be equally difficult to decide whether to sell at that point and cut your losses, or hold on to the stock in the hopes that it will reverse and allow you to recoup the money you have lost so far. Keep in mind, however, that holding on could potentially lead to even bigger losses. Below, let us take a look at how to sell your stocks.

Determine Why You Want to Sell

As a trader, the top reason for selling should be that your stock has hit your target price. Before getting into a position, you should have determined the price at which you will sell the stock. Once your stocks hit your target sell price, you can sell, since you will already have made your targeted profits. Having a target price can prevent you from making emotionally charged decisions, such as holding onto a stock for too long, which can wipe out your profits (and potentially lead to loss) in case the prices reverse.

Take Full Advantage of Time

There are ways in which you can make money in the stock market, even though you are there for the short-term. However, the real benefit of the stock market is its compounding effect, and that can only happen in the long run. The money that is present in your account will grow as the value of the assets keep increasing. This means that you are going to receive even more capital gains. So, with time, there is an exponential increase in the value of stocks.

Practice Investing Regularly

In fact, if you have a regular source of income, then you do not have to think about the payments – you can simply automate them, and they will be made on time. You can set a particular payment amount every week or every month.

Maintain a Portfolio That Is Diverse

Diversification is the key to make good profits in the market. There is a risk associated with every type of investment that you do. Sometimes, the companies that you are investing in now , might be underperforming in the course of one year. That is where diversification comes into play. If you do not invest all your money in one place, you will be safeguarding it against risks or challenges that come out of the blue or are unplanned.

Get Help From A Professional

If you are a beginner, you should consider taking some professional help, so that you learn and ultimately trade all by yourself. Trading platforms can help you do all the research, so that you are not wasting your time on trial and error. It is true that your chances of loss cannot be mitigated even when you are using professional help, but when you have an expert working with you, you will automatically feel better and more secure.

CHAPTER 15

How to Spot A Stock That Is About to Explode Higher

You need to perform **three fundamental steps** in order to find undervalued stocks:

Firstly, perform a preliminary evaluation of several stocks to see if they meet your investment criteria. **Secondly,** based on your preliminary evaluation, develop a shortlist of stocks that you want to further examine and evaluate. **Lastly,** perform a more detailed investigation of your shortlisted stocks by closely inspecting the companies' financial information.

The Internet has actually made it a lot easier for investors to acquire free financial information of companies that are interested to invest in. There are many websites now such as *Edgars* and *Sedar* that offer extensive databases of financial data, including audited financial statements, press releases, corporate reports, stock prices, and earnings per share.

However, given the barrage of information, how will you know if a particular stock is currently being sold below its inherent worth? Given below are just two of the financial ratios that you should look at, to assess a particular stock's inherent worth.

Price/Earnings (P/E) Ratio

You will soon hear financial analysts say that a particular stock is currently selling for 'x-times earnings', for e.g. 20-times earnings. This means the current market price of the stock is currently 20 times higher than the earnings per share of the company. The goal is to find stocks with very low P/E ratios because that means those companies are selling their stocks at lower prices.

Earnings Yield

Earnings yield is basically the opposite of P/E ratio. Therefore, a company with a 20-times earnings (P/E ratio) has a 1/20 or 5% earnings yield. If value investors are looking for low P/E ratios, the opposite applies with earnings yield (i.e. value investors are looking for stocks with higher earnings yield compared to other companies within the same industry.).

In addition to the quantitative assessments mentioned above, you must also perform qualitative assessments that allow you to better understand the intrinsic value of a particular company.

One of these qualitative assessments is the review of the company's 'insider purchasing activity.' You want to know what the company's executives (senior managers, officers, directors and other major stockholders) are doing with their stock ownerships.

These insiders, especially the senior managers and the board of directors, have inside information about the operations of their own company. Therefore, if you see them aggressively buying their company's stock, you can reasonably presume that the company's operations are moving towards a favorable future.

However, do not jump to quick conclusions when you see an insider selling his or her stock ownership. It does not always mean that the company is heading towards bankruptcy or harder times. For all you know that particular director or senior manager is in dire need of extra cash to fund his or her personal expenditures.

You can, however, begin to doubt the company's future prospects if many of the insiders begin to sell most of their stock ownerships. When you observe that scenario, you need to perform further investigations to see if the company is heading towards difficult times.

Now, you may ask, "How will I know when a company's board of directors or senior management is buying or selling their stocks?" Do not worry because the Securities and Exchange Commission (SEC) has made it easier for investors to find this information. Insiders are obligated to report their purchasing activities to the SEC within two business days after the transaction. You can then freely access this information through the official SEC website.

The Essence of Value Investing

You need to have the eagerness to do some serious reading and investigations if you want to be successful in value investing. You do not really need to have a degree in finance and accounting, but it will greatly help if you make the effort to learn about basic accounting, so that you can analyze and interpret financial statements properly. Remember that you do not decide to buy a particular stock because its financial ratios look promising or because you recently learned that its current market price has considerably dropped. In order to determine whether a particular stock is a good buy or not, you have to rely on more than simply taking in everything you see at face value. You will need to use your common sense and your critical thinking skills in order to be successful.

CHAPTER 16

How to trade momentum stocks

What are momentum stocks?

Momentum investing is one of the hardest of all the conventional trading approaches to define. Simply put, it is based on looking for companies whose stocks have been getting more potent over the last three months to a year. The rule is, "buy high, sell high."

Why People Choose Momentum Investing

Buying momentum stocks is proven to be an effective strategy. Two people credited with identifying momentum investing: Narasimhan Jegadeesh and Sheridan Titman. They showed that this strategy returns average returns of 1% monthly for the three to twelve months, following a given trigger occasion, that signifies when to buy the stock. Their first record was released in 1993 by the *American Finance Association*, and one more record that validated their earlier research study was published in the *Journal of Finance*.

The Advantages of Trading Momentum Stocks

The first benefit is profitability. Statistics show trading momentum stocks is a profitable strategy, provided you do your study and check your timing.

When choosing stocks, another advantage for some is that the system does not need absolute precision. Instead, momentum investors seek considerable incentives to take the chance of proportions. For every stock that loses a small quantity, they find at least one other several that generates a 50% or higher earnings.

Relative simplicity is one more benefit of this approach. Many trading systems need self-control, which many people simply do not have. The method of trading momentum stocks is entirely based on accurate information that is very easy to locate, so your emotions will not take you off course.

Many people assume the turnover in this way would be extremely high, but in majority of instances, it is not especially poor. Frequent turning over seems to be around 90%, and while steep, it is still less than with particular other strategies.

The Downsides of Trading Momentum Stocks

Momentum financiers do not buy stocks to hold. The stocks they hire are very unpredictable, and while the investors anticipate their momentum stocks to do well in the short-term, they are ready to sell as soon as the stock starts declining. That means if you do not get your timing right, you will not make much money.

Another complaint against the momentum trading is that economists cannot seem to figure out precisely how this technique works, which makes it look like it is based on nothing but dumb luck. Some financial experts think it works because the high returns offset the risk, while others assume it is an instance of smart investors taking advantage of the mistakes of other investors, such as overreaction to hot stocks.

Many stock investors know that momentum trading can be a profitable business. You can make large amounts of money in a short period.

That is why the essential aspect of momentum trading is the <u>understanding filter</u> you employ to make your buy and sell options. There are several superb stock systems and trading techniques out there; you need to evaluate them to uncover which ones help you the more. That is part of your research as a stock trader—test, test, and test again.

The worst point that can happen to a beginner momentum investor is to get information overload. It is better to evaluate a straightforward stock trading strategy step by step, that can show you how to focus on concrete plans to generate income and pick better hot stock trading opportunities once at a time.

Fortunately, there are good sites online today that can show you how to sell a sharp and efficient means.

This momentum trading is all about trading stocks according to your expertise FILTER. You can expect to begin making a considerable amount of money regularly when you know and follow your tried and tested filter specifications like a clock.

Momentum Stock Trading - Entry Points Are Tips to Earn from Momentum Trading

Momentum stock investment is the art of taking earnings from the stock exchange with short-term professions developed to benefit from the upward or downward day-to-day momentum of a stock's price. Lots of capitalists consider this to be a low-risk trading approach if done correctly. With self-control, you just enter a trade when the targeted stock's momentum is already relocating in your direction.

Establishing an entry factor above the current high (if you mean to go long) or below the current low (if you plan to go small) helps you catch bigger, much more substantial momentum in your professions. In our example, Stock XYZ was showing resistance at $60, i.e., the rate had not recently reviewed $60. I would establish an entry factor at something over $60, say $60.30. By setting your access factor over the most current resistance degree, your profession will only set off, given that the momentum is currently entering the instructions you predicted.

If, however, there is first descending momentum, your profession will not activate, and you have protected your resources for other trades. Setting proper entrance points is, as a result, necessary to your success in momentum trading.

How to Spot the Best Momentum Stocks

The stock momentum has a high turnover rate in the previous 3 to 12 months from the current day. Momentum investors typically hold a stock for a few months and check their holdings daily.

There are many stocks out there that accelerate in price and go on to make 100% to 300% returns in less than a year. Or perhaps in a few months.

Nevertheless, for the investors who are just beginning, momentum investing can be a confusing and discouraging experience to discover these stocks.

How to Sight Momentum Stocks

Among the things to find momentum, stocks are the relative stamina of the stock compared to the overall market over a given timeframe. A lot of momentum investors look at a stock that has outperformed at least 90% of all stocks over the 12 months. When significant indices decline, an excellent momentum stock exhibits strength by holding or perhaps exceeding their highs. When the significant indices rally, momentum stocks generally lead the rally and make new highs outmatching the market.

Possible momentum stocks ought to show in the equilibrium sheet that they are growing at a high rate.

Also, a favorable forecast by some analysts about the company's profits is necessary in identifying momentum stocks. Furthermore, momentum financiers also check out whether the reported incomes exceeded the experts' forecasts, quarter to quarter.

A business cannot expand its profits quicker than its return on equity, which is the company's earnings divided by the variety of shares held by investors, without increasing money by borrowing or selling even more shares. Some companies raise money by issuing stock or obtaining debt; yet both alternatives decrease earnings per share. For momentum investors, a potential stock ought to show a ROE of 17% or far better.

Meager trading quantities show the markets do not have an interest. Typically, momentum investors seek those with a minimum amount of 100,000 shares, or at least see their average everyday quantity increases as the value of the stock rises.

Start keeping a list of prospective momentum stocks and track their performance out there. With time, you will have the ability to spot the stocks that make up to 100% to 300% returns in a few months or less than a year.

Exit Strategies for Momentum Stocks

Over the last 16 months, a lot of stock markets have declined over 50%, and some private companies have been washed out thoroughly. The result of many portfolios has been devastating.

So, how does a financier or trader know when to sell?

Well, my point of view is of someone that focuses mainly on price and volume instead of the fundamentals of the underlying business. This market has clearly shown that the buy and hold technique can devastate your portfolio if you do not make use of a form of protection, such as choices, stock index futures, and shorting strategies.

Momentum Stock Trading - Stop-losses Are Essential to Capital Preservation

In momentum stock trading or any other approaches of day trading, a trader requires a means to decrease the risk of losing trades. Making use of stop-losses is crucial to an investor's resource conservation, in that stop-losses limit the size of a losing trade. A stop-loss is a pre-designated at a price at which a trader chooses to exit a business with very little damage.

There are two primary reasons to use stop-loss orders.

- Firstly, establishing a stop-loss help to manage your trading risk and maintain your capital for future trades. The reality for day traders is that not every trader is a winning trader.
- Stop-losses enable a small activity in the cost going against you but cap the quantity of adverse motion you are willing to soak up. By leaving a trade that is breaking you with only a little loss, you will have protected your trading capital for future professions.
- Secondly, stop-losses assist in eliminating emotional trading.

As an investor, you need to guard against being in a trade too long while wishing for a turnaround. Set correctly, your stop-loss will allow for small changes in cost but protect you from more effective momentum violating you.

How to Set an Effective Stop-loss

Let us use the following example. Assume my research reveals that Stock XYZ is poised to the run-up. It closed the previous day at $41.53, with a daily high for that day of $41.95. I generally establish an entry point at least $0.10 greater than the previous day's high. In this situation, my access point may be $42.05. Using a reward to take the chance of the proportion of 2:1, I would certainly put a stop-loss at $41.75 and an exit price of $42.65. This trading plan stocks a prospective benefit gain of $0.60 and minimizes any loss to $0.30.

When setting stop-losses, bear in mind to take into consideration a stock's current resistance levels in addition to a its recent trading activity.

Experienced day traders have found that about one in ten trades surpasses expectations, i.e., the stock's momentum carries the price beyond the targeted exit price. I advise using routing stops when this happens. In the above example, let us state that Stock XYZ exceeded our assumptions, going past $42.65. In this instance, I would change my stop-loss approximately $42.65 to secure in the first $0.60 of earnings and keep changing the stop-loss upward in $0.10 or $0.15 increments to 'trail' the higher momentum.

CHAPTER 17

Insider Tricks Used by Professional Traders

Maximizing Your Investments

Investors may maximize their investments by decreasing the cost of investing. There are several ways that investing may cost one money, and that money is coming directly out of the investment. Investors may switch from hiring a financial advisor to doing the investing themselves, cutting the costs of commission.

Retirement Plans

There are several savings plans that investors can get involved with. These can help to provide the investor with additional benefits that would not be available to them otherwise.

One of these plans is the 401(k). This is a retirement savings plan that will be sponsored by an employer. This will allow the individual to invest their money before taxes, so that they can save and invest some of their paychecks. The investor is not required to pay taxes until they withdraw this money from their account.

Do Not Follow the Crowd

When you decide to get into stock market investing, you must learn how to make decisions on your own. It is tempting to always listen to your broker or to listen to the friend who has been on the market for a long time. While it is just fine for you to take the advice of others when you are getting started, you must remember that this is your investment. No one else has money on the line when you pick a certain stock or go with a certain strategy. **Only you do.**

Pick Out A Strategy and Always Stick with It

As you should know by now, there are a lot of different strategies that you can work with when it is time to invest in the stock market. All of these strategies have the potential of making you money, but you need to make sure that you fully understand the strategy that you are working with. If you are not using the method in the proper way, you will not be able to make money.

Forget About the Timing

Timing the market is never a good idea. There are a lot of beginners who will try to figure out how to time the stock market, but they often end up losing a lot of money rather than earning anything. Experts in all industries agree that it is pretty much impossible to find the exact tops and exact bottoms of a stock; and if you happen to reach them, it was because you are lucky, not because of good planning.

Only Invest What You Can Afford

When you see a good investment opportunity, it is tempting to jump in and use all the money that you have. You may go out and use all your savings and some of the money from your paychecks this month in the hopes that it will turn out well and you will become rich. But what happens if the investment does not go the way that you plan? Now you have nothing, and you may not even be able to pay your bills the next month.

Keep Your Expectations Realistic

There are a lot of beginners who will join the stock market and hope that they are able to make a lot of money. They may hear that it is possible to lose money in this market; but they figure that they can outsmart the market, and that they will not end up losing all that much in the process. However, this is a bad way to enter the market. Even seasoned stock market investors who have been doing this for years will still lose money. There are many times when the market does something that you do not expect, and you can lose money no matter how much you plan.

Keep the Emotions Out of The Game

You also need to make sure that you are able to keep emotions out of the game. As soon as those emotions come into play, you will start losing money. These emotions will often lead you to make poor decisions, and you are more likely to lose out on your investment.

Set Your Stop Points

Another thing that you can consider doing is to set up some stop points. These are basically the points when you will exit the market, both when you are making profits and when you are losing. These can help to minimize your risks because you will make the decisions about these stop points before you enter the market and money is at stake. If you forget to do these, it can sometimes be hard to get out of the market at the right time, no matter how much logic you use.

Focus on Price

Taught traders follow a totally different arrangement of criteria. These traders' minds center around a solitary thought: cost. It might be an ineffectively run organization at the same time, if conditions require a concise improvement in its value, it is a decent buy for the broker who realizes when to get in and when to leap out for a snappy profit.

Practice Before You Jump In

This is ostensibly the most significant stock market nuts-and-bolts rule. Instead of investing in the wide market, you ought to think about after a couple of tickers and finding a workable pace trading range well indeed.

Always Have A Plan and Stick to It

You have to set rules on what qualifies as a good point to enter or exit a position. You must also set the strategy and budget that you will follow for your trades. Having these will help remove the emotions and create consistency in your trades.

Do Your Research

Due to the short time frame of a trader holding their position, the economic and financial aspects of a stock do not play a role in trading decisions. Technical and statistical analyses are more significant, sometimes the only considerations in making trading decisions.

Treat It as A Business

A business requires a commitment to succeed. This is the same for trading. Anything less would result in losses to a significant, if not whole, portion of your trading capital.

Be A Continuous Learner

Stock traders need to practice lifelong learning. They need to learn from the good and bad trades and see how they can improve upon it. They need to implement continuous improvements in their plant and test it before implementing it.

Do Not Risk What You Cannot Afford to Lose

The trading account should only contain funds that you can afford to lose. Do not put in funds allocated for personal expenses, the mortgage, your child's college tuition, and other personal expenses at any point in your trading career.

Always Use A Stop-loss

Any position you enter should have a pre-planned stop-loss point set at the same time as your entry. With this set, losses from bad trades are considered ahead of time.

Know When to Stop

If the plan is not working, you have to take a step back. Stop trading and see where it is going wrong. Do not return, unless you have found, created and tested a new trading plan.

Avoid the Herd Mentality

In most cases, the decision of many buyers is usually influenced by the actions of their close traders or friends. With this mentality, if everybody around you is investing in a particular stock, you are also likely to do the same.

Have a Financial Plan

Intelligent stock investment is not about getting rich quickly. Intelligent stock investing is a process that allows you, as an investor, to reach your set financial targets, through a financial plan that you have carefully crafted. This plan includes your financial constraints as well as a strategy targeting financial products, which in the process helps you to match your set goals with those financial constraints.

Be Clear on What to Buy and What to Sell

Once you have developed a financial plan, be keen to closely monitor ways with which different assets will perform in different macroeconomic conditions. Because we are dealing with stocks, it is good to know that stocks and commodities in most cases have been seen to rise with an expanding economy. Bonds on the other hand usually rise in an economy that is getting weak.

Stay Focused

Depending on the changes in the microeconomic and macroeconomic conditions, you can always adjust your portfolio selection as well as asset allocation basing on the products which you feel provides the advantage of one asset or stock category over another.

Develop in You the Intelligent State of Mind

As human beings, we have both intelligent and emotions guiding us in our daily actions. Because we have emotions, we come up with decisions using 'System 1' in the brain. 'System 1' is an automated mechanism in us that is controlled by our emotional feelings and intuition, and used for determining the exact action to be taken when responding to stimuli from the environment. It often relies on the assumption that the future is simply a repetition of the events that happened in the past.

Have a Trading Plan

When you have a plan, you set your goals way in advance, and you also know what it is that you exactly want from the trade. There are several advantages to having a trading plan, but the major one is that it gives you the chance to approach the trade with an objective mind. You will have greater confidence in yourself, and you can also keep your emotions at bay.

Make the Best Use of Technology

You have to keep it in your mind that the person sitting in front of you has all the latest technology at his/her disposal, and they are utilizing it to their full potential. Analyzing markets and viewing all the details is very important for making the right decisions, and charting platforms can help you do it the right way.

Keep a Check on Economic Calendars

I am going to tell you about a major trading secret that most people overlook, and that is keeping a check on the economic calendars. If you do this, you will be able to stay ahead of all the events that happen in the market and that have the ability to influence your trade.

Always Practice

You will not be perfect at something when you do not practice. Trading requires that you acquire and develop skills and strategies. Successful traders work hard and practice a lot. Time is usually the biggest teacher. Practice enables you to gain mental strength in trade. You should always practice every tip, every little skill that you gain.

Observe the Habits of Successful Trades

When it comes to trading, do not copy the trade strategies of another trader because this may work against you. Trading has many variables thus you will never copy the exact method that an individual use to trade and expect to win. It advised that you only observe the positive characteristics seen in successful traders and then cultivate these aspects in you.

Give Considerable Thought Before Choosing Your Trading Style

As you know already, there are different types of stock trading, and before you settle for any one of them, you have to think carefully whether that type of trading suits you or not. If you choose day trading, then you have to devote a fixed amount of time to trading on a daily basis. Then there is short-term trading, in which you can hold your position for a period of few days. You can also be a monthly or weekly trader depending on your time availability and effort you put in.

Choose the Right Broker

This is one of the most important steps, because there are a lot of things in trading that can be limited if your broker is not providing you with useful tools. If you do not want that to happen to you, then you have to make the right choice regarding a broker in the first place. However, before you move on to the decision of a broker, choosing your trading style is important because that is what will determine the broker too.

Do not Try to Outsmart the Markets

Here is a situation you have likely seen: an organization in a sector has an awful quarterly or interim review; all prices of stocks in that sector decrease despite the fact that other different companies have done nothing incorrectly. It is silly, yet that is the manner by which the market works. Also, fair company stock prices will go up in cost when the market is hot, in light of the fact that "a rising tide lifts all pontoons."

CHAPTER 18

Analysis of the stocks

Bull and Bear Markets

The stock markets often trend in one direction or the other. When the economy is faring well, interest rates are low and companies are thriving, then the stock markets will follow suit and thrive. When the markets thrive, it means the prices are generally going up. This upward trend is referred to as a bullish run and the market is said to be a **bull market**.

On the other hand, when the economy slows down, interest rates are high, and the outlook is poor, then the markets are likely to follow suit and stock prices will fall. This leads to a bearish run and the market is said to a **bearish market**. In the US, the markets have been on a bullish run since 2009. As such, most new traders have probably only experienced a bullish market but have never experienced a bearish one.

According to historic figures, bull market runs are often followed by bear markets. This is the norm as bear markets are also always followed by bull markets. The bull run that started in 2009 began just after a recession which happened in 2007/2008. Bull markets imply investor confidence in the markets while a bear market signifies a lack of confidence in the markets. The best part is that bull markets last for far much longer periods of time compared to bear markets. This is why it is possible to grow your portfolio over time, as the stocks are likely to overcome bear sessions.

Sometimes a stock market can experience a crash. This is a situation where stock prices drop drastically. This tends to affect the performance of different stocks but especially investor portfolios. However, another piece of good news is that a correction will take place and the markets will be restored. However, stock market crashes are pretty rate. When they happen, they do point to a possible bear market.

Therefore, as a potential trader, always think about researching before buying any stocks. Research is important and will mean the difference between success and failure. If you are unsure about the research, then you will be better off seeking professional advice. Your broker is one such expert. He can provide you with the advice that you need to invest wisely. However, this advice does come at a price and it will cost you. Plenty of experts believe it is much better and safer to pay for advice, rather than to take risks and possibly lose money. Therefore, seek advice where possible, and use it appropriately.

Fundamental Analysis

If you want to be a successful investor, then you have to learn about fundamental analysis. It is the most crucial aspect of any investment or trading strategy. Many would claim that a trader is not really accomplished if they do not perform fundamental analysis.

The fact is that it is such a broad subject that what it entails sometimes differs depending on scope and strategy. It involves a lot of things such as regulatory filings, financial statements, valuation techniques, etc.

Fundamental analysis can be defined as the examination, investigation, and research into the underlying factors that closely affect the financial health, success, and wellbeing of companies, industries, and the general economy.

It can also be defined as a technique used by both traders and investors to determine the value of a stock or any other financial instrument by examining the factors that directly and indirectly affect a company's or industry's current and future business, financial, economic prospects.

At its most generic form, fundamental analysis endeavors to predict and learn the intrinsic value of securities such as stocks. An in-depth examination and analysis of certain financial, economic, quantitative, and qualitative factors will help in providing the solution.

Fundamental analysis is mostly performed on a company to determine whether or not to deal in its stocks. However, it can also be performed on the general economy and on particular industries such as the motor industry, energy sector, etc.

The main purpose is to receive a forecast in order to profit from future price movements. There are certain questions that fundamental analysis seeks to answer. For instance, an investor examining a company may wish to know answers to the following questions:

- Is the firm's revenue growing?
- Is it profitable in both the short and long terms?
- Can if afford to settle its liabilities?
- Can it outsmart its competitors?
- Is the company's outlook genuine or fraudulent?

These are just a few examples of the numerous questions that fundamental analysis seeks to answer. Sometimes traders also want answers to questions not mentioned above. In short, therefore, the purpose is to obtain and profit from expected price movements in the short-term.

Most of the fundamental analysis is conducted at company level, because traders and investors are mostly interested in information that will enable them to make profitable decisions in the markets. They want information that will guide them in selecting the most suitable stocks to trade. As such, traders and investors searching for stocks to trade will resort to examining the competition, a company's business concept, its management, and financial data.

For a proper forecast regarding future stock prices, a trader is required to take into consideration a company's analysis, industry analysis, and even the overall economic outlook. This way, a trader will be able to determine the latest stock price as well as predicted future stock price. When the outcome of fundamental analysis is not equal to the current market price, then it means that the stock is overpriced or perhaps even undervalued.

Steps to Fundamental Evaluation

There is basically no clear-cut pathway or method of conducting fundamental analysis. However, we can break down the entire process, so that you know exactly where to begin. The most preferred approach is the **top-down approach.** We begin by examining the general economy followed by industry group before finally ending with the company in question. In some instances though, the **bottom-up approach** is also used, which is the opposite.

Companies are often compared with others. For instance, we may want to compare energy companies Exxon Mobil and British Petroleum. However, we cannot compare companies in different industries. For instance, we cannot compare a financial company like City Group with a technology firm like Google.

Determine the Stock or Security

You need to first have a stock or security in mind. There are many factors that determine the stocks to trade. For instance, you may want to target blue chip companies, noted for exemplary stock market performance, profitability, and stability. You also want to focus on companies that constitute one of the major indices such as the Dow Jones Industrial Average or S&P 500. The stocks should have large trading volumes for purposes of liquidity.

Economic Forecast

The overall performance of the economy basically affects all companies. Therefore, when the economy fares well, then it follows that most companies will succeed. This is because the economy is like a tide while the various companies are vessels directed by the tide.

There is a general correlation between the performance of companies and their stocks, and the performance of the general economy. The economy can also be narrowed to focus on specific sectors. For instance, we have the energy sector, transport sector, manufacturing, hospitality, etc. Narrowing down to specific sectors is crucial for proper analysis.

There are certain factors that we need to consider when looking at the general economy, such as the market size, growth rate, etc. When stock prices move at the markets, they tend to move as a group. This is because when a sector does well, most companies in that sector will also excel.

Company Analysis

One of the most crucial steps in fundamental analysis is company analysis. At this stage, you will come up with a compiled shortlist of companies. Different companies have varying capabilities and resources. The aim in our case is to find companies that can develop and keep a competitive advantage over its competitors in the same market. Some of the factors that are looked into at this stage include sound financial records, a solid management team, and a credible business plan.

When it comes to companies, the best approach is to check out a company's qualitative aspects followed by quantitative before checking out its financial outlook. We shall begin with the qualitative aspect of the company analysis. One of the most crucial factors is the business model of the company.

Business Model

One of the most crucial questions that analysts and others ask about a company is what it does. This is a simple yet fundamental question. A company's business model is simply what the company does to make money. The best way to learn about a company's business model is to visit its website and learning more about what it does. You can also check out its 10-K filings to find out more.

You need to make sure that you thoroughly understand the business model of each and every company that you invest in. Most companies have very simple business models. Take McDonald's for instance. They sell hamburgers and fries. At other times it is not easy to understand what a company does. For instance, the world's best-known investor, Warren Buffet, does not invest in tech companies because he simply does not understand what they do.

Competitive Advantage

We also need to take a closer look at a company's competitive advantage. Any company, that is to survive the long-term, needs to have a competitive edge over its competitors. A company with one such advantage has to be Coca-Cola because of the unique selling proposition. Others are Microsoft, Toyota, and Google.

Their business models provide them with a competitive edge that is hard for other to compete with.

In general, a unique competitive edge is where a company a company has clear trade-offs and options for customers compared to competitors, a unique product or service, reliable operational effectiveness and a great fit in all activities.

Management

Also crucial for any serious company is its management. Any company worth its salt has to have top quality management in major positions. Investors and analysts usually look at the level and quality of management to determine their competences, experience, strengths, and capabilities. This is because they hold in their hands the fate of a company. Even a great company with excellent ideas and plans can fail if the management is not right.

It is advisable to find out how qualified, experienced, successful, and committed the leadership of a company is. For instance, do they have prior experience at senior levels? Is there a track record and can management deliver on its stated objectives? These are crucial questions that should be answered appropriately for a positive conclusion.

There are plenty of tools available to the ordinary investor to learn more about the management of a publicly traded company. One of these tools is the company's website. Such a site is a trove of information regarding top managers such as the chief officers. You can also check out the conference calls where company c-suite executives host press conferences and present quarterly earnings reports. Many analysts await such opportunities to ask any questions they may have.

We also have the management discussion and analysis sessions that take place at the start of annual reports. During these instances, top managers often speak candidly about company's future outlook and things like that. Also watch out for corporate governance. This has to do with a company's guidelines and policies in place. It refers to the relationship that a company has with the management, stakeholders, and directors. You can find these guidelines and policies in the company's charter.

Effective corporate governance occurs where companies are able to adhere to their charters as well as all applicable federal and local regulations. Other factors that you should watch out for include the structure and constitution of the board of directors, the rights of all stakeholders, transparency, financial information, etc.

Industry factors

When conducting your company analysis, there are other factors that you will need to consider here. These factors include business cycles, the competition, growth in the industry, government regulation, and others. It is advisable to also understand the workings of a specific industry that you are interested in.

You should endeavor to learn more about the customer served by the said industry. There are companies that have millions of customers while others serve only a handful. A company that relies solely on a tiny number of customers for its revenue is considered a negative position and a red flag. However, companies with a large customer base stand a much better chance of doing well, if they sell to millions of customers across the board. Therefore, a firm with a large customer base is rated highly compared with one that sells to only a handful of buyers.

Government policy

In countries such as the United States, government policy is extremely crucial. When conducting fundamental analysis, you really should take this into perspective because certain policies can completely kill an industry. Companies provide relevant information on their 10-K forms which you can always look into.

Market share

Different companies within the same industry sometimes have to work hard to gain market share. There are sometimes a lot of companies fighting for a small share of customers especially at a local level. If a company controls about 85% of the market, then it means it is a solid company with strong fundamentals.

A strong market share also means that a company possesses that competitive edge over its customers. It also means that the company is larger than its rivals, and hence has a great future outlook.

Industry growth

This is also another aspect that should be taken into consideration. Some companies may have everything else working for them, but their future growth prospects may not be so bright. It is important to assess an industry and confirm whether there are any prospects for future growth.

Fundamental Analysis Example 2020

One of the world's best-known and most successful stock analysts is Warren Buffet. He uses fundamental analysis to determine which shares to buy and which companies to invest in. His success as an analyst has turned him into a billionaire.

Apart from analyzing companies, the equities market can also be analyzed. There are some analysts who conducted a fundamental analysis on the S&P 500 for a period of week. This was from 4th July to 8th July 2016. During this period, the S&P index went up to 2,129.90 points following the release of an impressive jobs report within the US. This was an unprecedented performance surpassed only by the May 2015 which was 2,132.80. The superb performance was attributed to the announcement of 287,000 new jobs across the country.

Technical Analysis

Technical analysis can be defined simply as a method, process, or tool that is used by investors to predict and foretell a stock's price movement based on data from the markets.

We can also define technical analysis of trends and stocks as the analysis of past market data that includes volume and price. The main purpose of the analysis is to obtain information that helps in predicting expected market behavior. Traders and investors believe strongly that precious stock price is a reliable indicator of future performance.

There is a notion that supports technical analysis. Apparently, the sale and purchase of stocks at the markets collectively by traders, investors, and other players is accurately manifested in the security. This holds then that technical analysis provides a fair and relative accurate market price to a stock or any other security.

The main purpose of technical analysis is to foretell the expected price movements of stocks and trends and to provide relevant information to investors, traders, and other market players to enable them trade profitably.

As a swing trader, you will apply technical analysis to the various charts that you will be using. You will use different tools on the charts to determine what the potential entry and exit points for a particular trade are.

Factors Affecting Technical Analysis

Technical analysis can be applied to numerous securities including forex, stocks, futures, commodities, indices, and many more. The price of a security depends on a collection of metrics, such as volume, low, open, high, close, open interest, etc. These are also known as **market action** or **price data**.

There are a couple of assumptions that we make as traders when performing technical analysis. However, remember that it is applicable only in situations where the price is only a factor of demand and supply. Should there be other factors that can influence prices significantly, then technical analysis will not work. The following assumptions are often made about securities that are being analyzed.

There are no artificial price movements: Artificial price movements are usually as a result of distributions, dividends, and splits. Such changes in stock price can greatly alter the price chart and this tends to cause technical analysis to be very difficult to implement. Fortunately, it is possible to remedy this. All that you need to do as an analyst is to adjust historical data before the price changes.

The stock is highly liquid: Another major assumption that technical analysis makes is that the stock is highly liquid. Liquidity is absolutely crucial for volumes. When stocks are heavily traded as a result of liquidity and volume, then traders are able to easily enter and exit trades.

Trend: If you are interested in trading based on trend, then what you are looking to do is follow the crowd when it comes to trading and make a profit on volume along with everyone else.

Examine the Charts

Experts advise investors to closely examine the chart of the stock they intend to buy as part of the technical analysis. When you examine the charts, you will be looking to spot the bottom and identify the best entry points. You will also examine the ceiling in order to identify the ideal exit points. Investors purchase stocks hoping the price will almost immediately go up. It is advisable to look at and understand historic chart patterns of the particular stock.

The buy point can be looked at as the ground floor of a building where an elevator is about to rise to new heights. It helps you to not only buy the right stock at the right price, but also at the right time.

Cup-with-Handle Pattern

One of the most powerful patterns that allow consistency with stock purchase is the cup-with-handle pattern. This is the point where you buy a stock at its lowest price and is likely to rise quickly. Human nature is still the same, where traders and other players in the markets exhibit either greed or fear.

This is defined as the price level where a stock is very likely to rise significantly. The buy point, also known as an entry point, is a point in the chart that offers the least resistance to price increase.

Example

Cup without a Handle

This is an approach that has worked over centuries. It is still believed to be among the most successful strategies for determining entry points. Let us take a stock that has seen its price decline by up to 33%. This is after a successful upward trend that showcased an all-time high.

However, before, the stock starts to decline for six weeks. Once the declining period is over and the upward trend begins, there are no signs of a major pullback. At this level, the entry point is pretty simple to determine. It is identified to be 10 cents on top of the peak towards the left-hand side. As soon as the stock recovers and gains 10 cents on top of the previous highest level. It is at this point that you enter the trade.

Past Price a Reliable Indicator of Future Performance

Traders understand basically that past price action of a stock and most other securities can help to accurately predict the future performance of the stock. This is why traders are always researching and analyzing past performance of various securities.

There are lots of other finance experts who rely on technical analysis and not just swing traders. We have analysts, investors, mutual fund managers, finance companies and others who use fundamental analysis followed by technical analysis thereafter. Technical analysis enables all these experts to narrow down to reliable, minimal risk entry price levels.

Charting Varying Time Frames

Future price movements can be accurately predicted using charts. There are different kinds of charts available with respect to a single security. There is the 5-minute chart, 15-minute chart, 1-hour chart, 4-hour chart, and finally, the daily chart.

There are primarily two variables at play when it comes to charting and technical analysis. These are the particular technical indicators and the time frames mentioned above. The time frame chosen by traders often reflects their personal trading style preferences. We have different kinds of traders: intraday traders, day traders, swing traders, long-term traders, and other investors among others.

How to Read Charts

There are numerous types of stock charts. Examples of these charts include candlestick charts, line charts, point-and-figure charts, open-high-low-close charts, bar charts and many others. These charts are viewable in varying time frames. For instance, we have weekly, daily, intraday, and even monthly charts.

There advantages and downsides of each chart type and time frame. They find application in different situations. What they reveal include price and volume action which are extremely important to traders and investors.

Why are Stock Charts Valuable?

When you find a share that you think has strong fundamentals, the next step is to its charts. The stock chart will provide you with useful insights that will guide you on the best time to enter a trade, how long to stay in the trade and when to exit.

Charts often plot both volume and price data in a format that is easy to read. This way, you can easily spot entry and exit points. Therefore, the key metrics to look out for are volume and price.

Stock Chart Interpretation

Price

On the stock chart above, there are magenta and blue colored marks. These marks represent the stock's price history. The volumes are also represented on the chart. The bars represent the price. The length of the vertical bars on the charts indicates a stock's price range. Therefore, the top of the bar indicates the highest price paid in that specific time period, while the bottom of the bar indicates the lowest stock price paid.

The tiny intersecting lines running horizontally point to the closing price at the end of the particular trading period. When the bar is in blue, this implies that stock price is equal to or greater than the previous price. However, it will be represented by magenta color if it is less than the previous price.

Volumes

At the bottom of the chart are vertical lines. These vertical lines represent the volume of shares trades within the indicated period of time. The height of the volume bars represents a value that is similar to that indicated on the right-hand side scale.

The color of the bars is determined by the preceding price bar. The bar color is blue if the price is greater than or equal to the previous period's last price. The color is magenta if the price is lower than the previous period's final price.

Moving Averages

Moving averages are indicated on stock charts in order to smooth out price data through the creation of one flowing line. This line basically represents the average price within a given time frame. Volatility is smoothed out by the moving average line. This makes it easier to spot points of convergence and divergence on a well-established price trend.

Traders and investors prefer to see moving averages that trend upwards. They also prefer to have a stock's current price closing higher than the training average. This way, a trader or investor will be confident that the stock is headed in the right direction.

There is a clear red line that cuts across the volume bars. This is another moving average line, specifically the 50-day moving average. The line is derived by dividing the volumes traded in the past 50 days by 50.

Comparing Stock Market Indices

Investors use stock market indexes as a general measure of how the stocks or securities markets are faring on any given day. Let us assume that you are a trader, and your portfolio of securities is headed south. If the indices are also on a downward trend, then you can assume that there is lethargy and pessimism in the general economy.

However, if your portfolio is underperforming while the indices are on an upward trend, then you may wish to reconsider some of your investments. The health of the stock market is often measured using different market indices. When the economy is faring well, the indices will rise. However, when the economy is depressed then the markets will follow suit and the indices will be on a downward trend.

Two Popular Stock Market Indices

The two best known and most popular stock market indices are the S&P 500 Index and the Dow Jones Industrial Average (DJIA). These two indices are popularly known as the securities market's benchmark. They are both important because they provide an indication of the wellbeing of the securities market. They also give traders and investors a historic basis that they can rely on to gain invaluable insights into the current state of the markets, and also derive useful data.

The DJIA is made up of 30 US companies with large market capitalization. The S&P 500 represents 500 major firms that have huge market capitalization and are usually selected by a committee. We also have the NASDAQ-100. This index consists of both US and international large cap firms but not any from the financial services sector.

How to Conduct the Indexes Comparison

1. Determine the indices you wish to compare.

We have observed that there are two major indices apart from NASDAQ-100. Each index fares differently; one may be down, while the others may be up.

2. Note that there are other smaller indices.

There are numerous types of stocks indices across the different markets. Some of the smaller ones include the Dow Jones Transport Average. Some are industry specific so choose carefully the indices you wish to compare.

3. Choose your preferred time frame.

Basically, the components of a particular index re likely to change based on a number of factors. The price is also likely to change so consider the time frame that you are interested in.

4. Check out charting sites and compare prices.

There are websites that contain the prices of different stocks and shares. Useful websites that you can visit include Yahoo Finance. You will get the information that you need regarding specific stock market indices. Other websites where you can find charts with indices include www.smartmoney.com, www.fool.com, and www.bigchart.com. Once you get to the charts, find the advanced chart feature for one index then enter the symbol of the index you wish to compare.

5. Check out the candlestick patterns.

Traders also use candlestick patterns as technical indicators. We can have a single candlestick or a combination of two or even three. Candlesticks are widely used indicators that enable us to observe potential trend reversals and market direction changes.

Candlesticks are formed based on the price action in a given period of time. For instance, if we have a candlestick based on a 5-minute chart, then it will demonstrate the price action for the specific 5-minute period. The same is true for the 1-hour and even 4-hour time periods.

There is an underlying principle when it comes to technical analysis. This principle dictates that the stock market price of a security represents all essential information that can have a significant effect in the market. Because of the availability of essential information, technical analysts see no need for fundamental or economic analysis. The opinion of technical analysts is that stock prices tend to follow trends.

They also believe that history tends to repeat itself, especially on matters of market psychology. There are two primary indicators that are popularly used by technical analysts. These indicators are technical indicators and chart patterns. Chart patterns are needed to identify areas of resistance and support. On the other hand, we have technical indicators which are basically a form of technical analysis. These technical indicators include moving averages which are among the most popular.

Looking at the market from the distance mainly refers to analyzing the trend of the market from the fundamentals of stock investment, including major macroeconomic emergencies and industry situations, etc.

CHAPTER 19

Possible Suggestion on How to Find A Profitable Stock Investment After the Pandemic

Analyze Your Stock Before You Buy It

It is important for you to analyze your stock carefully before your buy it. Do not rely on the things that you hear, and it is best to trust the information that you gathered yourself. It is advisable to learn how to conduct a fundamental analysis of the stock as well as technical analysis.

Fundamental analysis entails examining a company's financial statements or information to determine the fair value of the business stock, as well as gain insight regarding its future performance.

Fundamental analysis does not deal with company's recent movements in price, stock chart, or the performance of stock price over a particular period of time. Its main focus is the business itself. Fundamental analysis wants to find out whether the company's revenue grows, can compete well with its competitors, how much profit it makes, and how much debt it owes.

The main concerns of the analysis are the three past and present financial documents: the cash flow statement, income statement, and the statement of finance position.

Study the Company's Revenues

Studying the company's revenues over the past few years can give you an idea regarding where the business stands. Did it grow, decline, or remain stagnant?

You can use *Morningstar.com* to find the company's revenues. When you visit the site, type in your target stock, find your way to the tab, **Financials,** and then click on **Income Statement.** When you look at the top, you will find the company's revenues from ten years ago.

Ideally, you need to look for stable revenues that are bound to grow. Fluctuating revenues can tell you that the company is in a highly competitive industry.

Check the Company's Gross Profit Margin Or GPM

To get the profit margin, you need to get the gross profit first. You can get the gross profit by using this formula:

Gross Profit = Company's Earnings − (Raw Costs + Labor)

After doing that, you can calculate the gross profit margin using this formula:

$$GPM = \frac{\text{Gross Profit}}{\text{Total Revenues}}$$

Gross profit margin is expressed in percentage form.

For example, the company has revenue of $500,000, and $250,000 as its gross profits. When you divide 250,000 by 500,000, you get 0.5 or 50%, which is the GPM for this particular case.

Visit *Morningstar.com* to check out stable gross profit and high GPMs. Remember the below:

- A company with GPM over 40% all throughout is deemed strong.
- A business with 10% or less gross profit margin may be in an industry that is highly competitive, and does not have any power to establish high prices.

Note that the various industries have different margins. You need to compare margins of competing companies to get valuable information.

Analyze the Company Debt

A company with large amount of debt is something that you need to consider carefully. The company chooses to pay high interest rates because it is unwilling or lacks the capability to finance its growth using its available funds.

Understand that there are companies that choose to borrow large amounts of money to sustain their operations and still attain growth. They would rather borrow money than rely on investors. They use leverage and increase both potential risk and profits.

You can use debt-to-equity ratio to determine the amount of debt a company owes. You need to divide the debt of company by the shareholders' equity. The result helps compare which party (debt or shareholders) owns the larger part of the business. A low ratio of debt-to-equity is a good sign.

Evaluate Return on Equity (ROE)

ROE determines the kind of profits that a company generates using the stockholders' investment. You can obtain the ROE when you divide company's profit by equity of shareholders. *Morningstar.com* also provides information regarding ROE. You can find the equity on the Balance Sheet.

ROE above 10% is already considered strong, but you still need to compare your target company's ROE with its competitors, to make sure that you will not encounter unnecessary trouble.

Study the Company's Earnings Growth

An investor should be aware that whatever level of earnings growth a company may achieve, it would be the same with share price growth. That is why it is important to look at the past and future growth of the company. Take note that when we say earnings, we also mean profits.

When you visit *Morningstar.com*, you can look up the tabs, **Net Income** or **Earnings per Share,** to see past earnings growth over time. See if the earnings are steadily growing over time or declining.

You can use *Yahoo! Finance* to find the estimates on future growth of a company.

Find Out the Company's Price-To-Earnings (P/E) Ratio

This ratio can help you find out the amount that you pay for every dollar of profits. Divide the price per share by per share earnings to get the ratio.

The stock can be seen as expensive if you pay more for a dollar of your chosen company's profits as compared to that of its competitors.

For example, the stock price per share is $200 with $20 for every share as earnings. You will obtain a ratio of 10. It means a $10 payment is made for every dollar of your chosen company's earnings.

If the competitors of your chosen company obtain only a ratio of 5, your target company is deemed expensive.

Make A Comparison Table

Once you have fully analyzed the stock and calculated the P/E ratio, you need to prepare a comparison table between your target company and its peers. To be blunt, you need to look for a company or companies that outshine their peers based on the mentioned factors above. You still need to look for a company with a lower P/E ratio than its competitors.

For example, Company A and Company B both have gross profits of 40%, a return on equity of 9%, and steady growth for the past 12 years. However, Company A has a P/E of 14 while Company B has a P/E of 17. It is wise to invest in Company A, because you can get better business without costing so much.

You can go to *Morningstar.com* to search for a list of a company's competitors.

Great Stocks to Buy and Hold in 2020

After doing a careful evaluation and determining the companies that meet the criteria we have mentioned above, I think the following companies will offer strong risk-adjusted returns over the next ten years. You can also do a detailed analysis of them, and even add more to the list. But for now, these are good to get you started.

- Starbucks Corporation (SBUX)
- Brookfield Asset Management (BAM)
- Enbridge Incorporated (ENB)
- Texas Instruments (TXN)
- The Walt Disney Company (DIS)
- Discover Financial Services (DFS)
- The Travelers Companies (TRV)

CHAPTER 20

How the Market Will Suffer After Coronavirus and How They Can Get Back on Track

The stock market has millions of investors that may have opposing views. One investor may want to sell a particular security and another investor may want to buy it. Under certain circumstances, one investor may actually be losing money, while the other one may gain more than what he expects from the transaction.

You cannot explicitly say that the seller is the one who profits from the transaction and the buyer loses his money. Keep in mind that the value of stocks may fluctuate within the day.

The seller may actually be the one who will lose some profits from the transaction. It is possible for the price of stock that he wants to sell to go up in the next couple of hours. What if a clever buyer suddenly grabbed the opportunity and immediately buys it from him? The seller will no longer able to enjoy the profit that his stock should have given him, simply because it is no longer in his possession. The buyer, on the other hand, gets to reap all the profits in the end.

If you want to be a wise investor, you need to know more about the investment that perked your interest and study the market response to it. You should consider all the aspects of your target stock before you begin trading.

The Fluctuating Stock Prices

There are many things that affect the rise and fall of stock prices. The usual culprits are social and political unrest, natural disasters, supply and demand, and the absence of many suitable alternatives. There are times when media and the opinions of famous investors regarding certain companies or stocks can also affect the market.

These factors, together with the relevant information that has already been disseminated, may create a particular type of sentiment as well as corresponding number of sellers and buyers. If the number of sellers greatly exceeds the number of buyers, stock prices tend to go down. When there are more buyers than sellers, the price will surely go up.

Why is it Difficult to Predict?

Let us take a look at a scenario where stock prices have been rising for several years as an example. Investors know that sooner or later a correction will surely occur, that will bring the stock prices down. The day when the sale happens, triggers may be small, uncertain, even difficult to understand. There are investors who will patiently wait on the sidelines with their money in hand, and wait for the auspicious time before they dive in.

Those, who are more than willing to take the risk, may not hesitate to dive in because they already expect that the cash return is low, and they find it unbearable to earn nothing while seeing the stock prices get higher. This leads to a couple of questions. If you are the one on the sidelines, what signs do you need to watch out for, that will alert you when to get in? If you are already in, what are the signs that you need to see, that tell you that it is time get out? If it is easy to predict the stock market trend, then these questions should have never popped up.

There are actually three issues that a prudent investor should think about. The first issue is to understand the point in time when the stock prices have fair value. The second issue is to analyze the event that could cause possible downturn. The third issue involves learning the decision-making process of individuals. Take a look at the information given below, in order to see the big picture.

Stock Valuation

The market activity determines the actual price of a stock. A prudent investor often makes a comparison between the actual price of a stock and its fair value.

Take a look at this example: if a stock is being offered at $40 per share and its fair value is $45, you may actually gain a worthy purchase when you have decided to buy the stock. If it is being offered at $40 and its fair value is only $35, the stock could be considered overvalued. It is wise to avoid purchasing such stock.

What is the fair value of a stock and how do you compute it? Ideally, the computation is done using some standardized formula. But there are many ways to come up with the given figure. You can:

1. Combine the value of all the assets of the company, include it on the balance sheet, and subtract the liabilities and depreciation.

2. Determine the intrinsic value of the stock. You can compute the intrinsic value by determining the net current value of the future earnings of the company.

Triggering Event

It is advisable to know the events like the current coronavirus pandemic may possibly cause a trend reversal. A wise investor will always try to know or find out the things that are happening around him and the world, which may have an impact on his investments. You must be able to analyze things in order to arrive at a sound decision.

The Human Decision Process

This is the most interesting among the three issues. Each person has emotional and logical components. You may use your logical component to analyze a certain situation/event to help you come up with a sound decision. But when the time to finally make your decision, you may suddenly refer to your emotions to help you decide.

When making decisions regarding your investments, whether to buy or sell stocks, bear in mind that there will always be an investor who is interested on the things that you want to put up for sale. There are also investors who are selling the stock that you have wanted to purchase for so long. It is best if you can process the relevant data immediately and arrive at a good decision. However, you also need to understand that it is impossible to know all the things that you need to know and process everything without being biased. You might even end up making a sub-par decision. Such dilemma also occurs with individuals that are already considered the most analytical.

Important Reminders

As an investor, there are certain things that you need to keep in mind when dealing with stocks.

1. The stock market is rather complicated for a novice investor, but you will be able to grasp everything that you need to know within a certain time. Not every individual share the same level of understanding or aptitude.
2. It is best to avoid listening to the 'hot tip' that a colleague may have about stocks when he begins discussing it in the lunchroom.
3. There are different reasons that affect the rise and fall of stock prices. Some can be too complex to understand, especially by a novice like you.
4. When you invest, zero is the only sure bottom. You may want to include adding protection (i.e., options, stop orders, and others).
5. Always make sure that the stocks that you buy are truly worth your money.
6. Unless you are someone with penchant for taking risk, you may want to avoid putting all your money in one particular stock.

It usually takes years before you become well adept in dealing with financial markets and handling stocks. You may want to consider seeking help from a financial expert that you can trust, and who can take you under his/her wings to guide you properly. Venturing into the unknown territory alone may cost you more than you expect.

CONCLUSION

Pick up your necessities and get started on whatever it is you seek in creating wealth through trading in the stock market. If you find it challenging to engage in whatever you want, learning the basics, followed by understanding the essential guidelines are crucial. It does not have to be a gamble. By being clear on what your needs are, as well as the trading strategies available to you, you can put together a plan of action that can help you mix successful trades, not just once in a while, but basically every single time.

It all boils down to the learning curve. You have to stick to the learning curve. You have to learn what you need to, and take the necessary risks until you get the hang of it. Put in another way, if it was very easy then everybody would be a billionaire. Obviously, that is not the case. You have to stick to it, and you need to put in the time to learn what you need to learn, to develop enough expertise to at least trade profitably consistently.

Profitable trading, of course, means more than breaking even. Whether it is a dollar or hundreds of thousands of dollars, it is up to you. I wish you nothing but the greatest abundance and success in your trading.

Trading needs a great psychological power, because if you are unable to cope up with the losses you may entail you will give up. Sheer positivity and hope can make investors and traders succeed in very less time.

You can use different strategies to use your capital investment. It may take you some time to get settled in the arena. But when you get a hand on it there is nothing that can stop you. Now try to look at different stocks available in the market using any web app or mobile, and try to analyze using real time stock data. All the best for your trading career and always believes in optimism.

If you really want to succeed, you would have to read more about it and, hopefully, start practicing with a stock market simulator. After that, hopefully, you become more confident in getting started, open your first account with a stockbroker, and enter your first stock position.

The next step is to start practicing your stock trading skills, stock markets analysis, applying different strategies, and learn how to use the various financial tools, including chart-reading. All these are pretty simple and straightforward. If you put your heart and mind to it, then you will get to eventually learn and understand how the stock markets function.

It is amazing to learn that buying and selling stocks is a pretty simple affair. Most traders and investors, including novices, are able to pull this off. The main challenge will be to learn how to choose the winners. There are quite a number of stocks in all the different industries and sectors of the economy. If you learn how to identify the winning stocks, then you can expect your investments to grow immensely over the years.

As a beginner learning the building blocks, making necessary preparations, and following the needed steps, puts you on the forefront to achieve what seemed impossible in the stock market.

When mentioning the guiding tips for beginners, understand that there is a broad learning margin still out there; but having a clue about what you are to expect, prepares you for anything and everything that the stock market may throw at you.

NOTE OF THE AUTHOR

I hope this guide will serve you as a one of the many springboards that life will offer to become a successful investor. I would love to hear your honest feedback and I will now leave you with this quote that brought me inspiration :

"The best investment you can make, is an investment in yourself. The more you learn and the more you will earn." – Warren Buffett.

Made in the USA
Monee, IL
02 April 2021